The Windows Vista Book

Doing cool things with Vista, your photos, videos, music, and more

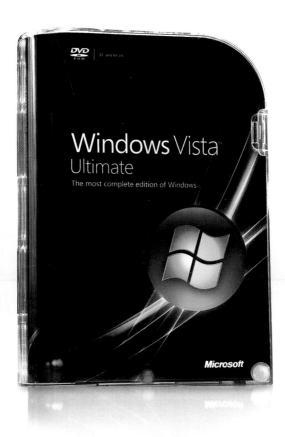

**Matt Kloskowski
and Kleber Stephenson**

The Windows Vista Book

**The Windows Vista
Book Team**

CREATIVE DIRECTOR
Felix Nelson

TECHNICAL EDITORS
Cindy Snyder
Kim Doty

TRAFFIC DIRECTOR
Kim Gabriel

PRODUCTION MANAGER
Dave Damstra

GRAPHIC DESIGN
Jessica Maldonado

COVER PHOTO BY
Matt Kloskowski

PUBLISHED BY
Peachpit Press

Copyright ©2008 by Kelby Corporate Management, Inc.

FIRST EDITION: April 2008

Composed in Myriad Pro (Adobe Systems Incorporated) and Lucida Grande (Bigelow & Holmes Inc.) by Kelby Media Group, Inc.

Trademarks
All terms mentioned in this book that are known to be trademarks or service marks have been appropriately capitalized. Peachpit Press cannot attest to the accuracy of this information. Use of a term in the book should not be regarded as affecting the validity of any trademark or service mark.

Windows, Vista, Windows Media, Windows Live, Xbox, and Internet Explorer are registered trademarks of Microsoft Corporation.

Warning and Disclaimer
This book is designed to provide information about Microsoft Windows Vista. Every effort has been made to make this book as complete and as accurate as possible, but no warranty of fitness is implied.

The information is provided on an as-is basis. The authors and Peachpit Press shall have neither the liability nor responsibility to any person or entity with respect to any loss or damages arising from the information contained in this book or from the use of the discs or programs that may accompany it.

ISBN 13: 978-0-321-50974-1
ISBN 10:   0-321-50974-9

9 8 7 6 5 4 3 2 1

Printed and bound in the United States of America

www.kelbytraining.com
www.peachpit.com

To my son, Justin, for always making me smile.
– Matt Kloskowski

For my mother, Barbara Stephenson—
you're everything a mother should be.
You're my hero!
– Kleber Stephenson

Acknowledgments (Matt Kloskowski)

Of course, there are many people behind the scenes that helped make this book happen. One of my favorite parts of writing a book is that I get to thank them publicly in front of the thousands of people who read it. So here goes:

To my wife, Diana: No matter what the day brings, you always have a smile on your face when I come home. I could never thank you enough for juggling our lives and being such a great mom to our kids.

To my oldest son, Ryan (my little golf buddy in training): Your inquisitive person-ality amazes me and I love the little talks that we have. Plus, the Nintendo Wii battles that we have give me just the break that I always need (even though you always win).

To my youngest son, Justin: I have no doubt that you'll be the class clown one day. No matter what I have on my mind, you always find a way to make me smile.

To my mom and dad: Thanks for giving me such a great start in life and always encouraging me to go for what I want.

To Ed, Kerry, Kristine, and Scott (my brothers and sisters): Thanks for supporting me and always giving me someone to look up to.

To my nephew, Jay Kloskowski, for being my biggest fan: Thanks buddy!

To my co-author, Kleber: Of course, I'd like to give a huge thanks to the guy that I knew for sure would help take this book to the next level. He's an amazing person with endless energy and enthusiasm, and he brings that passion to every book he writes. You're by far the Windows master (but I'll still take your money in a card game) and I feel privileged to have shared this book with you.

To the folks that made this book look so awesome, Felix Nelson, Jessica Maldonado, and Dave Damstra: Thank you! You guys are the best.

To my favorite editors in the world, Cindy Snyder and Kim Doty: Thanks for making me look so good.

To Paul Wilder, our in-house IT guru: Thanks for making sure I have a great computer and the software I need, when I need it.

I'd also like to thank Scott Kelby. In the years I've known you, you've become the greatest mentor and source of inspiration that I've met. More importantly, though, you've become one heck-of-a good friend. Thanks man!

To Dave Moser, my boss and my buddy: Your militaristic, yet insightful, comments throughout the day help me way more than you know. Thanks for continuing to push me to be better each day.

To all my friends at Peachpit Press: Ted Waitt, Scott Cowlin, Gary-Paul Prince, Glenn Bisignani, and your whole team. It's because you guys are so good at what you do that I'm able to continue doing what I love to do.

To you, the readers: Without you, well…there would be no book. Thanks for your constant support in emails, phone calls, and introductions when I'm out on the road teaching. You guys make it all worth it.

Thank you.

—*Matt Kloskowski*

Acknowledgments (Kleber Stephenson)

Debbie Stephenson: I've loved my wife since the very first time I laid eyes on her. She is stunningly beautiful. It's a ridiculous understatement to write that she's the most important thing in my life. My wife is perfect—from the color of her hair, shape of her lips, and sound of her laugh to the size of her feet. She's perfect to me. She's perfect for me. My heart still skips a beat every time I see her. You'd think that my infatuation with my wife would have worn off by now (after 13 years), but it hasn't. I don't think it ever will.

Jarod Stephenson: My little MX'er! I literally spend at least two weekdays each week recovering from my weekends. My son, Jarod, is a very big reason why. My little guy's killing me. ;-) Actually, I would never trade a single bump, bruise, back pain, contusion, or humiliating end-o for a single second. Riding motocross with my 9-year-old is my favorite thing. I am absolutely amazed every time I look at him. I'm not as talented, secure, tough, or fearless. I never will be. My son is the person that I most want to be like when I grow up.

Jenna Stephenson: My daughter is simply a miracle. It's as though God took every beautiful, extraordinary, fascinating, remarkable, breathtaking moment that he ever conceived and balled it all up into one perfect creation and named her Jenna. I'm completely blown away that Debbie and I, or any couple, would be able to bring something so special into this world. She's caring, loving, independent, headstrong, beautiful, and way smarter than I. She's exactly like her mother.

Kleber and Barbara Stephenson: It has taken me many, many years to come to terms with this, and although it pains me to admit that my wife has been right all these years, it's finally time that I 'fess up. Yes, I'm a "momma's boy." But, in my defense, if your mother was as wonderful as mine, you'd be one, too. She's my closest friend and confidante. Her guidance, love, and wisdom have influenced every aspect of my life. Being an understanding and loving parent to your children is the greatest gift you can ever give them. I've received this from mine in abundance.

My sisters: You might think that growing up with four sisters would have been tough…you have no idea! (Kidding!) My sisters are all so amazing, beautiful, successful, wonderful, fun, etc., etc., that I wouldn't know what to do without any of them. Cheryl Lucas, Kalebra Kelby, Julie Stephenson, and Heidi Crist are all so similarly exceptional that, if you didn't know them, you'd think they were a gifted cult of female intellectuals bent on taking over the world…hmm. ;-)

Matt Kloskowski: It was an absolute honor to co-author this book with Matt. Matt's an incredibly gifted writer and a genuinely great guy. Whatever success this book may have will be because of Matt and his efforts. Congratulations, Matt, on another great book from you!

Scott Kelby: Just when I think I'm brilliant, Scott reminds me that I'm not. It's always nice to have someone truly brilliant to remind you that you've got a lot to learn. Everyone in business should be as fortunate as I am to have someone that really does know it all, is always in your corner, and takes as much joy in your successes as his own. There are special people in this world that inspire others to be great, just by their example. Scott Kelby is one of those people.

Dave Moser: Chief…VIVA LA EMPIRE!

Kelby Media Group, Inc.: There has never been a more insanely talented group of people anywhere than the staff at Kelby Media Group. Every day they achieve stunning accomplishments. They do the seemingly impossible each and every day. I'd like to extend a very special thanks to my team: Alicen Rehnert, Viktor Garcia, Valli Vardas, Justin Finley, Kasey Carter, Angela Curtis, Debbie Stephenson, Dave Gales, Jeff Leimbach, Jamie Camanse, Rosemarie Ales, Phyllis Defrece, and Jackie Prince. Also, to the best book team on the planet: Cindy Snyder, Kim Doty, Dave Damstra, Jessica Maldonado, and the entire layout and production team. Thanks for your amazing efforts and hard work!

The Lord, Jesus Christ: Most importantly, to my Lord, Jesus Christ, thank you for giving me such a truly wonderful life. My life almost makes me fear Heaven…I just can't imagine an existence more perfect. As with all things in my life, I give you the honor, the praise, and the glory.

About the Authors

Matt Kloskowski

Matt Kloskowski is the author of 10 books on digital imaging and Photoshop, and his writing has simplified learning on the computer for thousands of people worldwide. Over the past 10 years, he's built a massive library of computer training videos (both online and on DVD) and magazine and online articles, has become host/co-host of three digital imaging podcasts, and has spoken at events worldwide.

Matt's concise, real-world, to-the-point teaching style has made him an industry go-to guy when it comes to learning on the computer. He is an Adobe Certified Expert in Photoshop and a Macromedia Flash Certified Developer. Matt resides in Tampa, Florida, where he works full time as an Education and Curriculum Developer for the National Association of Photoshop Professionals.

Kleber Stephenson

Kleber Stephenson is Executive Director of Training Services and Director of Windows Technologies for Kelby Media Group, Inc., a Florida-based software education and publishing firm. He's also the author of the best-selling *Windows XP Killer Tips* and *Microsoft Office 2003 Killer Tips*, from New Riders Publishing, and co-author of *The iTunes for Windows Book*, from Peachpit Press.

A contributing technology reviewer for *Photoshop User* magazine and *Layers* magazine, Kleber has nearly two decades of experience analyzing and implementing business computing infrastructures based on the Windows platform. In addition, he has designed and developed real-world network and administrative solutions based on Microsoft technologies and the Windows OS architecture.

Kleber lives in the Tampa Bay area of Florida with his wife, Debbie, his son, Jarod, and his daughter, Jenna.

Table of Contents

Table of Contents

Table of Contents

Chapter 5   91

Surfing the Web
Getting Online Quickly & Safely

Table of Contents

Table of Contents

Table of Contents

Introduction

You know what? We can't stand introductions. I know, it's a bold statement coming from a couple of authors, right? But it's like some committee got together and said that you've got to have an introduction in your book. Oh, and please make it long. Really long, and really boring! In fact, make it so long as to ensure the fact that no one ever reads the introduction in your book, or any other one for that matter. And the vicious cycle begins. However, we do understand the concept of an introduction. It's for the author (or authors) to introduce you to the content of the book and give you an idea of how best to get the most out of the book you just purchased. We'll do that, too, but we're going to do it with a very short list (we love lists, by the way). Here goes:

1. Who is this book for? It's for anyone that has Windows Vista, and just wants a quick, easy way to get up to speed on making it useful. It's not for people that like to read the techie-weenie stuff about kernel errors and command line prompts, though. It's for people that don't have a lot of time and just want to be able to jump in, read a few pages, learn something quickly, and then go try it out at the computer.

2. Feel free to read the book in any order you want. We organized the book in a way that seems logical for what most people want to do. But jump in wherever you want. Hey, it's your book. You bought it, right? You're smart enough to realize that if you want to learn about email, then go to Chapter 6. If you'd rather learn about how to organize your music, then skip right to Chapter 8.

3. If you haven't noticed, there are a few different editions of Windows Vista. One of the biggest issues we've found that people run into is simply not knowing if a certain feature is supported in their version. Well, we've made it really easy for you in this book. At the bottom of each page, you'll see colored dots (light green, dark green, blue, and black). They're not just eye candy, they actually mean something. Each colored dot corresponds to an edition of Vista.

 Home Basic

 Home Premium

 Business

 Ultimate

Here's how they work: If you're not sure whether a tip you just read works in your edition, look at the bottom of the page for the dot that corresponds to your version. If it's in color (not grayed out), then it works for your version. For example, let's say I have the Home Basic edition and I just read a tip. I look down at the bottom of the page and see this graphic:

As you can see, the Home Basic dot (light green) is grayed out, so that means the tip doesn't work in my version.

This doesn't happen often, though. This book is mostly applicable to all versions of Vista, and if you flip through the pages right now, you'll see there aren't many grayed-out dots at all. So, no matter what edition you have, you'll find plenty of cool tips here.

4. Every once in a while, you'll notice a tip in a box at the bottom of a page. It looks kinda like this:

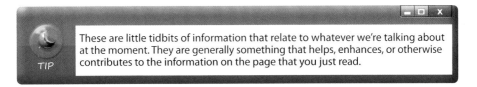

TIP

These are little tidbits of information that relate to whatever we're talking about at the moment. They are generally something that helps, enhances, or otherwise contributes to the information on the page that you just read.

That's it. That's the introduction. Easy. Simple. Short. Now get to it, and enjoy the book. Oh…and thanks for reading the introduction (that no one reads). Enjoy the rest of the book.

Matt & Kleber

CHAPTER ONE

Vista's Coolest Features

Top Ten Things to Do Now, If You Just Can't Help Yourself

If you're the impatient type, then this chapter was tailor-made for you. In and of itself, Windows Vista is a worthy upgrade, and you'll see little benefits here and there for months to come. Plus, there's a ton of stuff under the hood that you'll never see that makes your computing experience better and safer. However, if you bought this book because you're brand new to Vista, and you just want to know what's in it for you, then try out these 10 things to really give you that instant gratification feeling.

Tabs in Internet Explorer 7

One of the coolest features in Vista comes in the Web browser—Internet Explorer 7. IE7 has this feature called tabs that lets you open multiple websites all in one Web browser window. It's absolutely perfect if you like to do 10 things at once (like check stocks, visit eBay, shop on Amazon, check the news, etc.). Instead of opening up multiple browser windows and cluttering up your desktop, you can just open multiple tabs in the same window. To try it out, launch IE7 by going under the Start menu and clicking on IE7 at the top left. Type in a Web address to visit a site. If you look toward the top of the window, you'll see a tab that shows the site you're visiting. Right next to it, you'll see an empty tab. Just click on that empty tab to open a new blank page. Then type in another address to visit another site, and the tabbed madness begins. You can find out more about IE7 in Chapter 5.

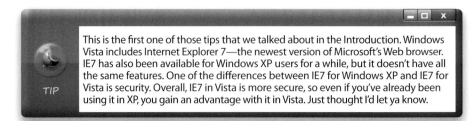

TIP

This is the first one of those tips that we talked about in the Introduction. Windows Vista includes Internet Explorer 7—the newest version of Microsoft's Web browser. IE7 has also been available for Windows XP users for a while, but it doesn't have all the same features. One of the differences between IE7 for Windows XP and IE7 for Vista is security. Overall, IE7 in Vista is more secure, so even if you've already been using it in XP, you gain an advantage with it in Vista. Just thought I'd let ya know.

See Everything That You Have Open at Once

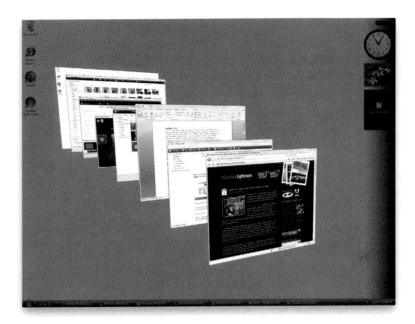

Flip 3D is one of the first visual features that you can start using right now. It's a quick, easy way to see your open programs visually. Just press the Windows key on your keyboard and then press the Tab key. This brings up a 3D window of each open program and what your current view of that program looks like. Holding down the Windows key and pressing the Tab key repeatedly will cycle (or flip) through each open program. When you see the one you want, let go of the keys and that program will be brought to the front. You can find out more about Flip 3D in Chapter 2.

Using Gadgets to Quickly Get to the Things You Need Most

Gadgets are so darn cool that we could easily spend a chapter on them (actually we did—check out Chapter 3). In a nutshell, gadgets are little mini programs that give you information or allow you to access cool tools without opening a bunch of larger programs. So, if you wanted to check the weather, see your calendar, and access a calculator without opening up three separate programs (Internet Explorer, Windows Mail, and Calculator), then gadgets are the way to go. The easiest way to get started with gadgets is to Right-click on the Sidebar (that's new to Windows, too) and choose Add Gadgets. This opens the Gadgets dialog and shows the gadgets you have installed on your computer. Just click on one and it'll appear in your Sidebar, ready for action. They're always there, so you don't have to go looking around for them in other windows. You can find out more about gadgets and the Sidebar in Chapter 3.

Instant Search

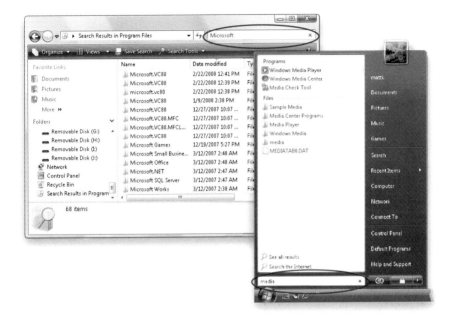

One feature in Windows Vista that rocks is the desktop search. Any time you have a Windows Explorer window open, a search box appears in the upper-right corner. From there, you can search for any kind of file or information on your computer. Just type it in—no matter what it is. It doesn't end there, though. Searching capability is literally everywhere you look. For example, you can use the search field that's built into the Start menu to find/launch any application easily. Just type in the name of the program, click on it to select it from the search results, and then press Enter to launch it. This is way better than navigating through a nested menu like you do in Windows XP. You can find out more about searching in Chapter 10.

Organize (and Fix) Your Photos with Photo Gallery

Windows Photo Gallery is a brand new program that only comes with Vista. What is it? It's the new place that all of your photos will live. To launch it, go to the Start menu and choose Windows Photo Gallery (if you don't see it here, go to All Programs). Once you've got the program open, you can import your photos and organize them so you can find the ones you need quickly. You can also fix your photos with some neat adjustments to lighten them and even make black-and-white images. Finally, it has some cool sharing features like launching your favorite photos directly into a slide show. There's actually so much to it that it's got its own chapter. Check out Chapter 7 to find out all the things that you can do in Photo Gallery.

Aero Look and Feel

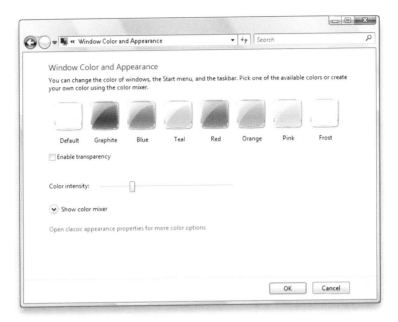

Aero is the brand new user interface in Windows Vista. Basically, it's a whole new look, feel, and experience that makes it easier and more fun to use Vista. Part of this look and feel is the glass-like appearance that the windows now have. It's just easier to look at. Plus, it's totally customizable, so you can change the colors to suit your taste. To enable or modify the Aero settings, Right-click on the desktop and choose Personalize. At the top of the window, choose Window Color and Appearance. Once you're there, you can start making changes to the color and transparency of your windows. To find out more about Windows Aero, check out Chapter 2.

TIP

Aero is only available in the Home Premium, Business, or Ultimate editions of Vista, however there won't be a tip like this every time this is the case. Instead, there are those little dots at the bottom of the page that are color-coded by version (see the Introduction for more on this). That way you can see if the feature listed on that page is only available in a certain version(s) of Vista.

Back Up and Restore

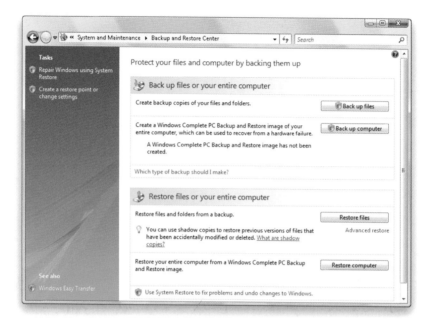

Back up your computer now. If you do it right after you read this tip, you will have paid for the price of this book and even your upgrade to Vista in one shot. To back up, go to the Start menu and choose Control Panel. Look under System and Maintenance, and click the Back Up Your Computer link to open the Backup and Restore Center. So why am I so fanatical about this backing up thing? I'm telling you from experience that I used to think it would never happen to me, but several computer crashes later, I've become a backup freak. It used to be a lot harder in Windows XP, but Vista made a huge leap forward. You can even back up to an external hard drive and schedule backups to happen automatically. Put that together with a restore feature that's really easy to use and you have one of the best new features in Windows. Do it! Back up—now. What are you waiting for? You can find out more about backing up in Chapter 4.

Live Icons

In Windows XP, your icons used to only depict what type of file it was. In Vista, though, your icons now mean something more. They can actually show what a file contains. What this means is that you don't have to open a file to see what's in it. Instead, enabling live icons lets you see a thumbnail preview of the content of a file. It's great for photos, because you don't have to open the photo to see if it's the one you want. You can even see the first page of your documents. To use Live Icons, go to a Windows Explorer window, click on Views in the menu bar, and make sure you have either the Small, Medium, Large, or Extra Large Icons selected (you'll probably need the Large or Extra Large Icons settings to really make this one work).

Faster Resuming from Sleep Mode

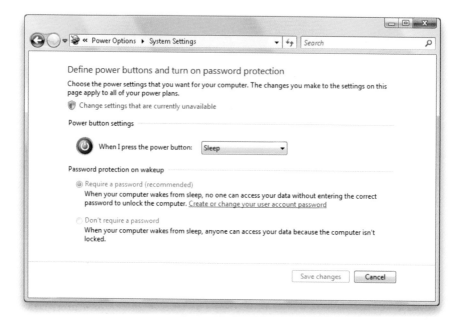

I'll start this one by just telling you that Sleep mode actually works in Vista, and I bet I'll hear cheers from all over. If you ever used it before, you feel my pain as well. Hey, I just call it how I see it, and Sleep mode in Windows XP was flat-out lame. If it did ever work, it took forever to resume from, so, you might as well have just rebooted. Well, Vista makes Sleep way better. The way it works is this: The new default "off" mode for your computer is Sleep. This means when you press the power button on your desktop or laptop, the computer goes into this super-ultra-power-saving mode. It saves everything you were doing before it went to sleep onto the computer's hard drive. Then when you press the power button again to awaken your computer, it comes out of Sleep mode and every-thing resumes like normal (and it does it quickly). It's really useful if you have a laptop and you're trying to conserve battery power, but it's also something that's good to do with a desktop, say, right before you head to bed for the night.

Parental Controls

If you're a parent, then this feature is a must-have. At this point, you don't need a lecture as to why we need parental controls. Instead, I'll just tell you how to turn it on quickly and get started. To turn parental controls on, go to the Start menu and choose Control Panel. Then, click on the User Accounts and Family Safety link. Under Parental Controls, click on the Set Up Parental Controls for Any User link. The only trick is that you'll need to create your own user account for each child, but that's really easy to do. Once everything is all set up, you'll be able to monitor the time your children spend on the computer, which websites they visit, and even get reports on their computer usage. You can find out more about parental controls in Chapter 5.

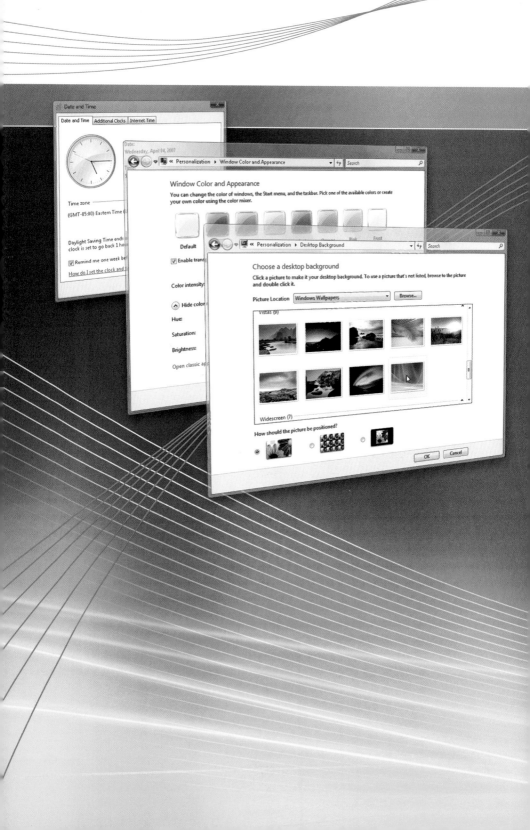

CHAPTER TWO

Customizing Display and Appearance
Making Your Desktop Feel Like Home

People are visual. We like big, pretty pictures. Some of us more than others, but we all still like things to look cool. Throw in the fact that most folks like personalization and you have the very makings of a new chapter—one dedicated to customizing all of your display and appearance settings in Windows Vista. There's a brand spanking new user interface, so (if your version of Vista supports it) you're going to see some very different-looking windows on the screen. Everything still pretty much works the same, it's just way more sleek and pleasing to the eye than Windows XP.

What Is Aero?

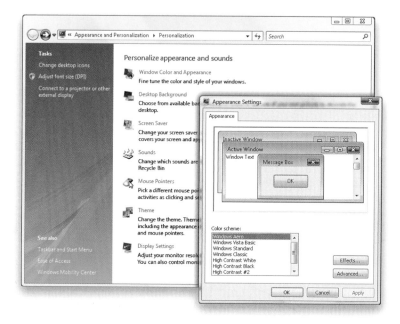

Aero is a word Microsoft uses to describe the new user interface look and feel in Windows Vista. If your computer meets the minimum standards for running this interface, the windows and buttons you'll see will have this cool glassy look to them. When you use this interface, which by the way is turned on by default, you'll see that your windows are translucent, your dialogs seem to expand open instead of just appearing onscreen, and even your buttons appear to have this plastic/glassy look to them. Even better, they glow when you hover over them. So why is this important? Well, it contributes to an overall better user experience. The whole interface is much more pleasing to look at and it creates a very open, lightweight environment. This, in turn, helps you focus more on your work and less on the surrounding interface.

Does Your Computer Support Aero?

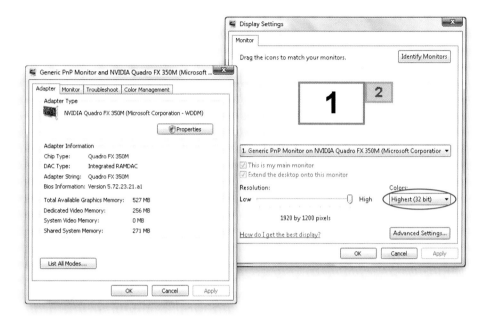

If you're not sure whether your computer supports Aero, then here are the system requirements (they mostly deal with your graphics card):

- Windows Display Driver Model (WDDM) driver
- Pixel Shader 2.0
- 32 bits-per-pixel color
- Adequate graphics memory:
    - 64 MB of graphics memory to support a single monitor at a resolution lower than 1,310,720 pixels
    - 28 MB of graphics memory to support a single monitor at a resolution of 1,310,720 to 2,304,000 pixels
    - 256 MB of graphics memory to support a single monitor at a resolution higher than 2,304,000 pixels

If your system meets the above requirements and has 512 MB of system memory, you can enable Windows Aero by going to Start>Control Panel>Appearance and Personalization> Personalization, and changing the Theme to Windows Vista and the Color Scheme to Windows Aero (click on Open Classic Appearance Properties for More Color Options at the bottom of the Window Color and Appearance dialog). If you're not sure, you can always call your computer manufacturer and give them your computer model. They'll be able to tell you whether it can run Aero or not.

What's New with the Start Menu?

The Start menu hasn't undergone a total facelift, but it does have a few changes that make it easier to use. First off, you'll notice that there's a little search field at the bottom so you can quickly find files and folders without going too far. As you type in your search terms, the results show up right in the Start menu instead of opening another window. The right side of the Start menu is dedicated to some quick links to frequently used folders and areas in Vista. The actual program list area, which you're probably already used to, works better in that the folders expand within the list itself (hover over All Programs to get to it). No more large, unwieldy folder expansions that take up your whole screen. If you get too far into a folder, then you can always just click Back at the bottom of the Start menu to get back to the original program list. Finally, there's a better way to turn off your computer. Just click the little power button that appears at the bottom right of the menu to save your current work and programs just as they are and then put your computer into a sleep mode that uses less power but lets you start back up quickly. Finally, if you click the little right-facing arrow to the right of the power button, you can perform various things like logging off, switching users, or even powering down the computer altogether. Overall, the new Start menu is a good thing. It's got enough new stuff there to keep you busy and make it easier to use, but it's not so far removed from the old Start menu that you have to learn how to use it all over again.

Setting the Date and Time

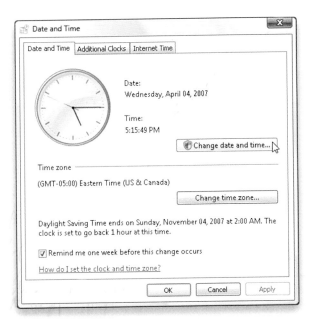

To get to the date and time setup in Windows Vista just click on the Start button. When the Start menu opens, click on Control Panel on the right side, then in the Control Panel, click on Clock, Language, and Region to get to the page that lets you manage your date, time, time zone, and regional settings. Under Date and Time, go ahead and click on Set the Time and Date to open the dialog above. Then, just click the Change Date and Time button to view a clock and calendar that you can edit. Enter your new date and time info and click OK. Click OK once more to close the Date and Time dialog, and your new date and time settings will take effect. Keep in mind that you can also set Windows to automatically synchronize with Internet time (it is set this way by default). To do that, in the Date and Time dialog, click on the Internet Time tab and click the Change Settings button. There you can turn auto synchronization on or off, as well as change the Internet time server you want your computer to synchronize to.

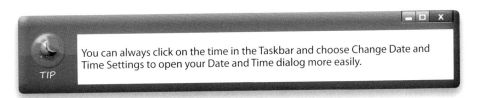

TIP

You can always click on the time in the Taskbar and choose Change Date and Time Settings to open your Date and Time dialog more easily.

Adding a Clock for Another Time Zone

Vista makes it simple to track the time in other time zones. Say you have family or friends that live in Tokyo, Japan, and you communicate with them often. It can be a pain to always do the math to figure out what time it is there, so you can set up another clock. Just like when setting your date and time, go to the Start menu, click on Control Panel, then click on Clock, Language, and Region. This time, instead of clicking on Set the Time and Date, choose Add Clocks for Different Time Zones instead. This opens the dialog shown above. The first thing you'll need to do is turn on the Show This Clock checkbox. Then, select the time zone that your friends or family are in from the Select Time Zone pop-up menu. Once you find the time zone, type in a descriptive name for the clock. Something like "Tokyo Time" or "Flippy and Franky's Time" will do just fine. On the off chance you don't have two friends named Flippy and Franky, feel free to substitute your own names. You can add up to two clocks in this dialog. Just click OK when you're done. Now, when you hover your cursor over the time in the Taskbar (or click on it), you'll see the time in Tokyo as well.

Installing a Font

If you've never had to design a presentation, poster, brochure, or newsletter, then you may very well have never thought about fonts. A font is essentially a complete set of characters you use to type. There are lots of different styles available. By default, Vista will have plenty of fonts for you to sink your teeth into for various looks and feels. However, you may find one that you just absolutely need to have. Many fonts are available for purchase, but there are also many free fonts for download. Either way, once you download the font, you need to install it. To do this, go to the Start menu and click on Control Panel. In the Control Panel, click on Appearance and Personalization. Under Fonts, click on Install or Remove a Font. This opens the window you see above. All of the files you see in there now are the fonts you have on your computer. To install a new font, Right-click anywhere on the right side of the dialog and choose Install New Font. In the Folders section of the Add Fonts dialog, navigate to the place where you stored the font you just downloaded. You'll see the potential fonts found appear in the List of Fonts section at the top. Press Install and Vista will automatically install the font for you.

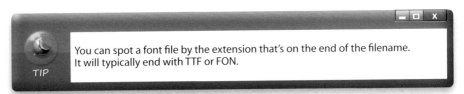

You can spot a font file by the extension that's on the end of the filename. It will typically end with TTF or FON.

TIP

Setting the Number of Recent Apps

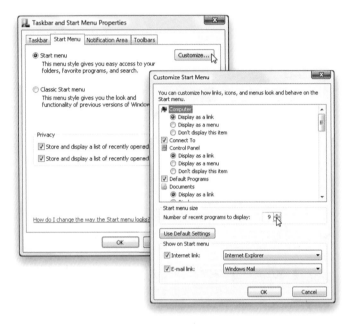

By default, Vista remembers which applications you've opened recently. This helps in a lot of ways but mainly when it comes to speed, because most people use the same programs over and over again. You'll be able to get to the programs you use the most right in the main Start menu where Vista stores them. Vista automatically remembers the last nine programs you've used. Just click the Start button and you'll see them on the left side. Now, if you use more programs than that regularly, you may run into the issue that some of your recent apps get knocked off the list because another one has been added. Or, you may not use that many and you want to reduce the number of programs Vista stores. Either way, you can change the number of recent applications by clicking on the Start button to open the Start menu. Then, Right-click in an empty area on the left side and choose Properties. On the Start Menu tab, click the Customize button to the right of the Start Menu option at the top. This will open the Customize Start Menu dialog. About halfway down, you'll see the Number of Recent Programs to Display setting. Just bump that setting up or down by clicking the small arrows to change the number of recent programs you want Vista to remember, and click OK. Click OK again to close the dialog, and your Start menu will now show the number of recent programs you just chose.

Adjusting the Overall Volume

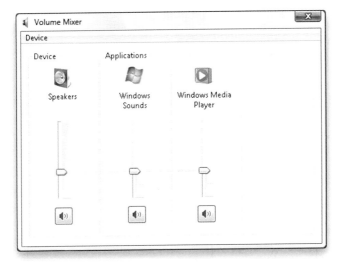

Whether you're giving a presentation and you'd like to increase the volume so everyone in the room can hear or you'd just like to pump up the volume to jam out to your
music, you'll need to know where to find it. In Vista, you adjust your volume by going
to your Control Panel via the Start menu, then choosing Hardware and Sound. On the
Hardware and Sound page, under Sound, you'll see Adjust System Volume. Click on
that to open the Volume Mixer dialog you see above. Then adjust the Speakers volume
slider to your liking. Moving it up makes the sound louder; moving it down makes the
sound softer. You can also adjust the overall volume of the sounds that Vista makes as
well as the volume used in Windows Media Player here.

Changing Your Mouse and Cursor Movement Speed

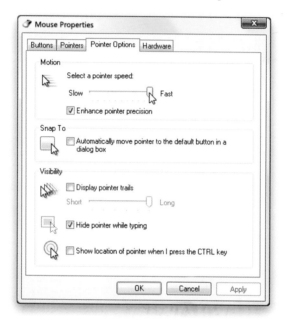

I've got to say that whenever I sit down to a new computer this is absolutely one of the first things I do. I can't stand it when my mouse doesn't move fast enough across the screen. Or, worse yet, it zips across the screen at the speed of light and I can't find it. So, if you're like me, it's good to know where to go to adjust this type of behavior. All of your mouse settings are reached by going to the Start menu and choosing Control Panel. Now, your computer sees a mouse as hardware so, as with most hardware settings, you'd naturally go to the Hardware and Sound section. However, some settings are so common to change (like the mouse) that you can reach them right in the Control Panel Home section. Under Hardware and Sound you'll see the Mouse option, so go ahead and click on it. This opens the Mouse Properties dialog shown here. As you'll notice, there are a heck of a lot of tabs here. Seriously, who knew there were that many settings for a mouse? Since we're only concerned about the speed here, click on the Pointer Options tab at the top. Under Motion, set the pointer speed to your desired speed. I typically bump this all the way to the right because I like my mouse to move fast. If you prefer slower movement, then you'd move yours to the left. You'll also see the Enhance Pointer Precision checkbox, and it should be turned on. When would you not want your mouse to be precise? I'm not sure, but if you did, this is where you'd go to turn the option off.

Automatically Opening a Program When Vista Starts

Everyone has programs they use all the time. For me, it's email and a Web browser (and Photoshop, too). When I start Windows, the first thing I do is open these programs. Like XP, Vista has a way to automatically open a program when you start Windows. The first thing you need to do is go to the Start menu, choose All Programs, and locate the Startup folder. Right-click on it and choose Open. This is where you will put things you want to automatically start up when Windows boots. The next step is to find the programs you want to automatically start. Press Ctrl-N to open another window, and use the folder view on the left to navigate to the folder your desired auto-start program is in (most of your programs should be in the C drive under Program Files). Once you find the program folder, double-click on it and locate the EXE file that's used to launch the application. Right-click on it and choose Create Shortcut. You may get an alert telling you that Windows can't create the shortcut there and asking if you'd like to create it on the desktop. If that's fine, click Yes; if not, it'll create it right there. Either way, you'll see a new icon appear. Drag that icon into the Startup folder and now it'll automatically open when Vista starts.

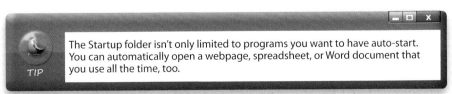

TIP

The Startup folder isn't only limited to programs you want to have auto-start. You can automatically open a webpage, spreadsheet, or Word document that you use all the time, too.

Using the Quick Launch Toolbar

The Quick Launch toolbar is one of my favorite things to customize in Windows. If you're not familiar with it, it's located right next to the Start button. Because of its name, it doesn't take a rocket scientist working for NASA to figure out that you quickly launch things from this toolbar. To show the Quick Launch toolbar, just Right-click on an empty area in the Taskbar. From the contextual menu that appears, choose Toolbars, then choose Quick Launch. You'll see it pop up next to the Start button already populated with some programs that you'll frequently use. To launch one of those programs, just click once on its corresponding icon. That's it. Seriously, I have to say this is one of the most frequently used areas in Windows for me since I store all of my favorite programs there.

Adding More Programs to the Quick Launch Toolbar

Okay, if you're reading this then the Quick Launch toolbar has become near and dear to your heart as well. Because you've come to like it so much, you've probably thought to yourself that it would be great if you could add more programs to the Quick Launch toolbar instead of the ones that Windows has chosen for you. Well it sure must be your lucky day, because guess what? You can! Just click on any program you'd like to add (don't release the mouse button, though) and drag it over to the Quick Launch toolbar. Just like that you've added a new program to it. If you're not sure where to find the programs, you'll typically find everything you need in the Start menu, or even on your desktop, since lots of software programs like to install shortcut icons there, too.

TIP

You're not restricted to programs in the Quick Launch toolbar, though. You can drag-and-drop your favorite documents there as well, so they're always just a click away.

Tweaking the Quick Launch Toolbar

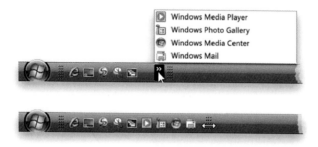

I know what you're thinking: Matt, you've gone a little overboard here. You're saying to yourself, it's only the Quick Launch thingy (that's tech speak for toolbar), right? Do we really need another page dedicated to this? Yes, we do. I think it is just *that* cool. So here are a couple things you can do to tweak the Quick Launch toolbar. First, as you add more programs to it, you may start to notice it becoming a little unwieldy. When this happens, Windows will put a handy little double-arrow thingy (there's that word again, but it doesn't mean toolbar this time) next to it because it can't fit all of the programs you've added. To me, that arrow thingy defeats the purpose, so I just click-and-drag the toolbar sizing handle (that's the little dotted separator bar) to the right. Keep dragging it until you can see all of your programs. Now, one more trick. If you realize that you don't want something in your Quick Launch toolbar, just Right-click on it and choose Delete. That will remove it from the toolbar but not your computer. It will still reside wherever it did in the first place.

Adding New Items to the Taskbar

The Taskbar isn't like the Quick Launch toolbar. You can't really add programs to it manually. You can open a program and it'll appear in the Taskbar, but when you close it, it's gone. However, you can add more toolbars to the Taskbar. Just Right-click on an empty spot in the Taskbar, choose Toolbars from the contextual menu, and you'll see a submenu of items you can add. Before, we added the Quick Launch toolbar, so if you did that, it should have a check next to it. However, you can also add something like Windows Media Player to the Taskbar. Go ahead and choose that one and when you open Windows Media Player and Minimize it, you'll see a new toolbar appear. Here you can control Windows Media Player using a mini control system just like you would if the full-blown window was open. To remove an item from the Taskbar, just Right-click on it again, go under Toolbars, and uncheck any you want to get rid of.

Previewing Your Open Programs

Preview thumbnails are a brand new feature in Windows Vista. If you see a bunch of open programs along the Taskbar but you're not sure what one of them is, just hover your cursor over that program in the Taskbar. These are also called Taskbar thumbnails and they'll give you a mini view of what the program window looks like. Plus, they work with video programs as well, so if a video is playing you'll still see a live mini preview.

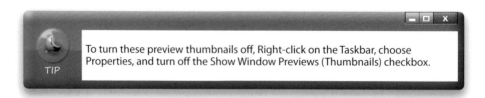

TIP

To turn these preview thumbnails off, Right-click on the Taskbar, choose Properties, and turn off the Show Window Previews (Thumbnails) checkbox.

Interacting with the Taskbar

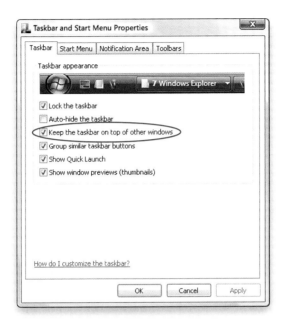

What you do here really depends on how much you want to interact with the Taskbar. If you'd like the Taskbar to stay put and never move (this can happen a lot if you accidentally click-and-drag on it), then try this. Right-click on an empty area in the Taskbar and choose Lock the Taskbar. Now you won't be able to move it or change anything on it. Another choice you have is to keep the Taskbar over all other windows or allow windows to be dragged on top of it. Right-click on the Taskbar and choose Properties. Then take a look at the Keep the Taskbar on Top of Other Windows setting. If you leave it on, then you won't ever be able to drag a window over the Taskbar. If you turn it off, you'll be able to move windows so they obstruct the view of the Taskbar.

Hiding the Taskbar

You can also force the Taskbar to get out of your way when you're working by auto-hiding it. Right-click on the Taskbar again and choose Properties. Then turn on the checkbox next to Auto-Hide the Taskbar. Now the Taskbar will dip out of the way when you're not using it. Once you move your cursor over the bottom of the screen, the Taskbar will ease back up again for you to interact with it. When you're done, it'll hide again.

Making the Taskbar Larger

If you find you always have a lot of programs open and the Taskbar looks cluttered, you can always make it larger. Just click-and-drag upward on the topmost part of the bar (make sure that Lock the Taskbar is not on). You'll see a little double arrow, and if you drag up, the Taskbar will add more rows to it to make it easier to see your open programs.

Getting Back to Your Old Start Menu

If old habits die hard for you and you just want to get back to your old Start menu, you can. However, I highly recommend against it. You've spent the money and gone through the trouble of upgrading to Vista. You've probably been using Windows XP for years now, so why not take a break from that old Start menu? But if you absolutely feel the need to go back, you can. Right-click on the Start button and choose Properties. This opens the Taskbar and Start Menu Properties dialog. On the Start Menu tab, you'll see an option for Classic Start Menu. Just click on that radio button and you're set. You can even customize it if you'd like by clicking the button to the right. Again, I say stick with Vista's slightly revised, but cooler, Start menu. Even if it's a little weird at first, it'll grow on you.

Creating Shortcuts on Your Desktop

There's another way to get at your favorite programs more easily. You can store them on your desktop as shortcuts to the original. First, go to the Start menu and find the program you want to create a shortcut to. When you find it, Right-click on it and choose Send To. Choose Desktop (Create Shortcut) and that'll place an icon on the desktop that will take you right to the program if you double-click on it. Now keep in mind, it didn't move the program to your desktop, it just created a shortcut. So if your desktop becomes too cluttered, you can always Right-click on that shortcut icon and choose Delete to remove it.

TIP

This tip doesn't just work for programs on your computer. It works for any files or documents, as well. Say you have a favorite Microsoft Excel spreadsheet or Word document that you use often. Just open Windows Explorer and find that file. Right-click on it and choose Send To>Desktop (Create Shortcut), and you'll have a shortcut that points to that file on your desktop for easier access.

Adding New Items to Your Start Menu

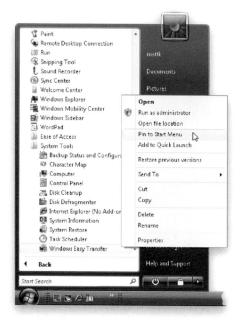

Yep, there's yet another way to quickly get at your favorite programs. I find this one is useful for those programs that I use every few days, but not all the time. I put the ones I use all the time in the Quick Launch toolbar, but I don't put too many in there because it gets too crowded. Instead, I do this: Open the Start menu and navigate your way to a program that is buried three folders deep and just a pain in the neck to get to. When you find it, Right-click on the program and choose Pin to Start Menu. That puts a shortcut to the program icon at the top left of the main area in the Start Menu. So, whenever you open the Start menu from now on you'll see the program there ready to launch. If you ever need to remove it from the Start menu, just Right-click on it and choose Unpin from Start Menu. Like all of the shortcut tricks we've seen so far, this is just a shortcut to the main program, so you're only deleting the shortcut, not the whole program itself.

Changing Window Colors

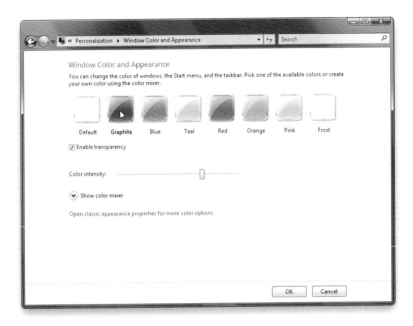

I've got to warn you, I'm a total sucker for anything visual. Give me a way to customize the look and feel of my computer and I'm doin' it! That said, here's a great tip for totally customizing your Windows interface and making it any color that you want. Using that Windows Aero technology we talked about earlier, you can change the color theme of all of your windows. Right-click on the desktop and choose Personalize. At the top of the window, click on Window Color and Appearance. In this new window, you can do some pretty revolutionary stuff when it comes to making your computer your own. Across the top are a group of thumbnails that show the various colors you can change your interface to—just click on one and Windows will automatically change everything and show you the new color. Now that is cool. Not only do the windows look cooler in Vista, but you can change their color too. As far as color choices go (you knew I had to chime in here on this one, didn't you?), it seems Microsoft lumped the, shall we say, more masculine colors toward the left and the more feminine colors toward the right. That's not to say that if you're a woman you can't pick Blue—you can pick whichever color you want. And if you're a man, you can even choose Pink if you'd like (but prepare to be mocked beyond all belief by your friends and co-workers).

Customizing the Color of Your Custom Color

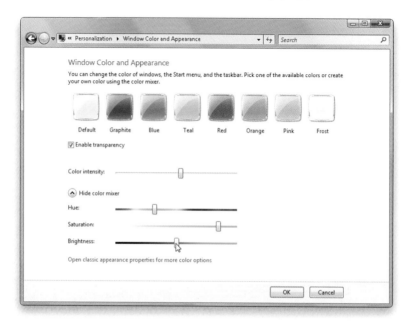

Okay, I realize I just showed you how to customize the color of your windows. However, there's more to it. Yep, I was holding out on you. You can also customize the color you chose. Yep, just go back into your Window Color and Appearance window and look at the option that reads Color Intensity. Moving this slider to the left or right adds more or less of the current color that is chosen above. That's not it, though. Right below that you'll see a small down-facing arrow for Show Color Mixer. Click on the arrow to expand that section and you can mix your own colors. The sky is the limit here. If you can mix it, you can have it as your window color. Use this in conjunction with the Color Intensity slider and now you've got some really kick-butt ways to get some more color into your windows.

TIP

If you've ever changed your color to the point where you can't stand it and want to get back to the way things were, just click on one of the color thumbnails up top. Those actually never change regardless of the changes you make in the Color Mixer, so you can always get back to the way things were.

Turning the Transparent Windows On and Off

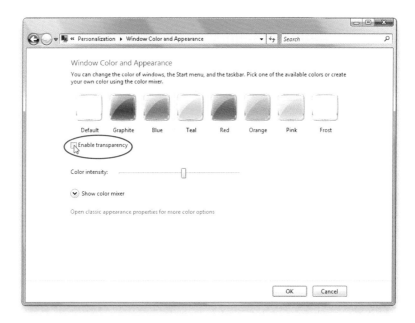

Like I said earlier, I'm a sucker for visual changes. Another one of those cool new Aero features is the way you can see through parts of your windows to whatever is below them—those in the know call it transparency. Original name, isn't it? Anyway, I personally like this feature, but you already knew that. However, if you don't like it and find it distracting, you can indeed turn it off. Right-click on the desktop and choose Personalize. Then click on Window Color and Appearance. Right below the color thumbnails (which is another really slick way to customize your windows) is a checkbox for Enable Transparency. Turn it off to turn the transparency off. If you ever realize that hey, that Matt guy was right and windows do look much cooler with transparency, then just go back to the same place and click the checkbox to turn it back on again.

Changing Your Desktop Background (a.k.a. Wallpaper)

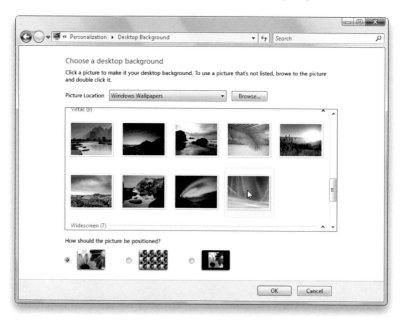

Just like in Windows XP, Vista lets you change your desktop background. Right-click on the desktop and choose Personalize. Then, click on Desktop Background near the top of the window. You'll see a bunch of photo collections (Black and White, Light Auras, etc.), each with a little arrow on the far-right side that lets you collapse and expand the collection to see the images in it. To choose a background, just click on one of the thumbnails. Yep, that's it. You can also select one of the built-in sample images, any image in your Pictures folder, or a solid color background by choosing a new picture location from the pop-up menu. If you want to add one of your own images that isn't in a folder on the Picture Location pop-up menu, click the Browse button to locate it on your hard drive, click on the image, then click Open.

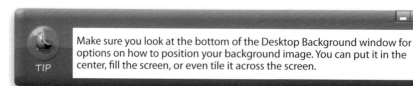

TIP

Make sure you look at the bottom of the Desktop Background window for options on how to position your background image. You can put it in the center, fill the screen, or even tile it across the screen.

Setting Your Monitor Resolution

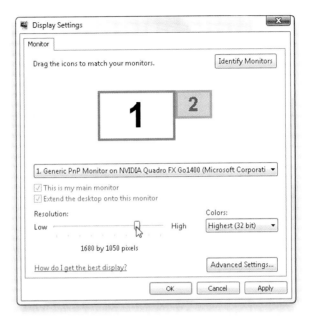

Your monitor (also called a display) resolution determines how much stuff you see displayed on your screen. It's measured in horizontal and vertical units called pixels. The lower the resolution, the less you'll see on the screen; the higher it is, the more you'll see on the screen. In Vista, you can change this setting by Right-clicking on the desktop and choosing Personalize. Click on Display Settings at the bottom of the window. Toward the bottom of the resulting Display Settings dialog, you'll see a Resolution setting. Drag the slider somewhere between Low and High to your desired resolution setting and click OK.

TIP

If you've got a laptop or LCD monitor, be careful here. Most laptop displays have a sweet spot that is predetermined by the manufacturer. That sweet spot is what's called the "native" resolution. You can change it, but doing so will often make your windows look fuzzy and less clear. It's best to check with the manufacturer to see what the recommended resolution of your screen is and use that.

Turning on the Screen Saver

Screen savers used to have an important purpose when it came to the life of a monitor. If one thing was left on the computer too long, then it could actually burn into the screen permanently. Nowadays though, that really isn't a worry. However, screen savers do serve a couple new purposes. One is for security, and the other is that some of them just look cool. As far as security goes, they're helpful if you get up from your computer and forget to turn the display off. If your computer doesn't detect anything going on, then it'll turn the screen saver on. You can control the time that Vista waits to turn the screen saver on or disable it altogether by Right-clicking on the desktop and choosing Personalize. Then click on Screen Saver. In the Screen Saver Settings dialog, you can preview the different animations available by choosing one from the Screen Saver pop-up menu and clicking the Preview button to the right. Right under the Screen Saver pop-up menu, you'll see a Wait setting. That's where you tell Vista how long to wait for inactivity before it kicks the screen saver on.

Putting Your Display to Sleep

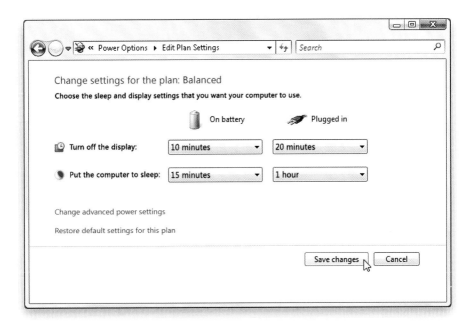

Wouldn't it be great if you remembered to shut your monitor off every time you got up from your desk and walked away? While displays don't eat up that much energy, they still do use it and why leave your screen on if you're going to be away for a long period of time? You can have your display automatically turn off after a certain amount of time by Right-clicking on the desktop and choosing Personalize. Choose Screen Saver (I know, it doesn't really make sense, but trust me) and look at the bottom of the dialog. You'll see some blue underlined text that reads Change Power Settings. Go ahead and click it to bring up the Power Options window. On the left side of the window, click on Choose When to Turn Off the Display. In the next window, you can tell Vista how long to wait before turning off the display when your computer is plugged in and when it's running on battery power (if you have a laptop that is). After you make changes, just click the Save Changes button to close the window and Vista will remember your new settings.

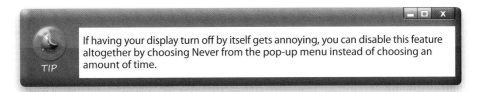

TIP

If having your display turn off by itself gets annoying, you can disable this feature altogether by choosing Never from the pop-up menu instead of choosing an amount of time.

Putting Your Computer to Sleep

Sleep mode got a bad rap in Windows XP because it was a little quirky and no one really knew when it would work or not. It's been totally revamped in Vista, though, and works beautifully. Essentially, sleep mode is when you turn the power off on your computer. By default, it'll automatically go to sleep. Everything that is currently in use will be saved to memory (RAM and hard drive) and Vista will turn everything off except for a few key items. It's a great way to save power when you're away from your computer. To use it, just press the power button on your computer. You could also go to the Start menu and click the right-facing arrow all the way over on the bottom-right side and choose Sleep.

TIP

If you're on the desktop and no programs are in front, you can press Alt-F4 to bring up the Shut Down Windows dialog and choose Sleep from the pop-up menu there.

Switching Visually Between Open Programs

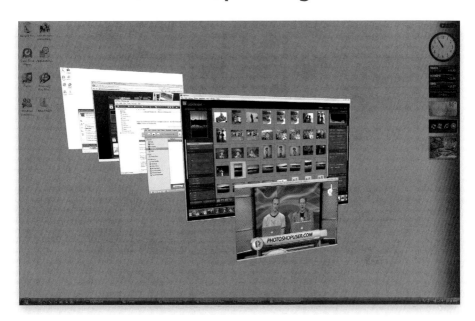

Vista has this sweet new feature called Flip 3D. It's a visual way to flip through all of your open programs so you can pick which one you want to go to. The old way to do this was by pressing Alt-Tab. This showed a quick icon list of the open programs in the center of the screen, but you really couldn't see which was which unless you knew exactly what the icon looked like. That shortcut still works, but now in Vista there's a better way. You can press the Windows key and the Tab key. This brings up a 3D window of each open program and what your current view of that program looks like (even videos will show up). Holding down the Windows key and pressing the Tab key repeatedly will cycle (or flip) through each open application. When you see the one you want, let go of the keys and that program will be brought to the front.

CHAPTER THREE

All New Gadgets and Sidebar
They're New. They're Cool. Find Out How to Use 'Em

Gadgets and the new Sidebar are probably my favorite new features in Windows Vista. They almost make the price of the upgrade worth it by themselves. What's a gadget, you ask? You'll find out more in the coming pages, but, in short, a gadget is a little tiny program that runs in your Sidebar and gives you access to lots of information—like stock quotes, emails, contacts, eBay auctions, and just about anything else you can think of—right at your fingertips. They stay right there as you're working, so all you have to do is glance over at the Sidebar and get your instantaneous information fix.

What Is a Gadget?

Gadgets are mini-applications that let you do common things like check weather, stocks, and news, as well as many other things. They give you fast access to information and put the things that you want to know right at your fingertips. It's hard to compare gadgets to anything that you've seen before in Windows, though. The best way I can explain them is this: think about how convenient it would be to have all the information from your favorite websites right at your fingertips. That's what gadgets do for you. One thing you should know: gadgets are very much Web-based so you'll typically need to be connected to the Internet to use most of them. (We'll talk about a few that you don't need an Internet connection for later.)

Why Should I Use Gadgets?

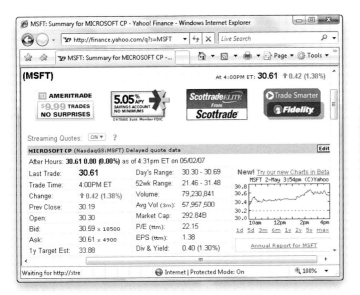

One of the questions I've heard folks ask is why they should use gadgets. After all, for the most part gadgets provide the same information you can find on the Internet and your favorite websites. Here's my take on why you should use them: while gadgets provide much of the same information you can find on the Web, there is one key difference—they're not on the Web, they're right in front of you. So picture this: You're working at your computer and you decide you'd like to know what your favorite stock's price is at the moment. Before gadgets, you had to open or switch windows to your Web browser and get to your favorite stock website. If you're the organized type, then you probably had the site customized to show you your stocks. If not, then you had to type in the stock symbol to get the latest price. That's life before gadgets. Now jump to Vista and life with gadgets. Again, you're working at your computer and you decide you want to check your favorite stock. So you just glance over to the side of your screen to the Sidebar, and there it is. That's it. You're done. You don't have to stop what you're doing and switch gears to something else. Everything you need is right there. That, my friends, is why you should use gadgets. And trust me, once you start using them you'll be hooked, and you'll be downloading all kinds of new ones to play with (more on that later).

What Is the Sidebar?

Think of the Sidebar as the home for gadgets. Gadgets need some place to live, and that's where the Sidebar comes in. It's located on the desktop and it keeps your gadgets all in one organized place instead of spread all over your desktop. The Sidebar is on by default when you install Vista. It shows up along the right side of your screen. In fact, it already has a few gadgets preinstalled in it so you should be able to find it easily. If, by chance, you don't see the Sidebar, then just go to your notification area at the right side of the Taskbar and look for the little Sidebar icon (it's blue with a couple icons on the right side and if you hover over it, the tip reads Windows Sidebar). Click on it and the Sidebar will pop open along the side of your screen. It doesn't stop there, though. You can customize the Sidebar to suit your needs. That's on the next page, though.

TIP

If you've lost the Sidebar altogether, then go to the Start menu and choose All Programs. In the Accessories folder, click on Windows Sidebar. That will go ahead and open the Sidebar for you.

How Do I Get Started with Gadgets?

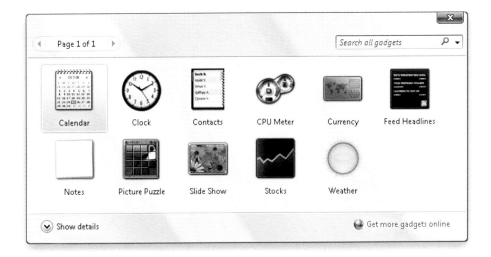

Vista includes a bunch of gadgets to help you get started, so just Right-click on the Sidebar and choose Add Gadgets. This opens the gadgets dialog and shows the gadgets you have installed on your computer. If you've got a lot of gadgets, you'll see a page number in the top left of the dialog. Just click the Right or Left Arrow keys to page through the gadgets. If you're not sure what your gadget is called or what page it's on, then you can use the Search field at the top right of the dialog.

Adding a Gadget to the Sidebar

Adding a gadget to the Sidebar is really simple. Open the gadgets dialog by Right-clicking on the Sidebar and choosing Add Gadgets. Then click-and-drag a gadget from the list in the dialog onto your Sidebar. The gadget will appear in the Sidebar ready for you to use or customize. Go ahead and try it. Let's use the Weather gadget as an example. Right-click on the Sidebar and choose Add Gadgets. When the dialog opens, click-and-drag the Weather gadget from the dialog over to the Sidebar and it'll appear there ready to use.

TIP

You can also double-click on a gadget in the gadgets dialog and it will automatically appear in the Sidebar ready for duty. Or (as if you needed another way to do it), you can Right-click on the gadget in the dialog and choose Add.

Customizing the Sidebar

As you'd imagine, the Sidebar can be customized. After all, we all use our computers differently. To customize the Sidebar, Right-click on an empty area within it and choose Properties. The Windows Sidebar Properties dialog you see above will open. Here you can do a few things. At the top, you can control whether the Sidebar will start automatically when Windows starts. Right below that is a checkbox for Sidebar Is Always On Top of Other Windows. This is one you'll want to be familiar with, since it has a big effect on the way you use the Sidebar. Personally, I turn this option on. That way, the Sidebar will always remain on top of my windows and make it easy for me to see the information I want quickly. If you leave this option off, then you'll just have to move any window that is in front of the Sidebar to see your gadgets. A couple of the other options include which side of the screen to display the Sidebar on and which monitor (that is if you have multiple ones) to display the Sidebar on. If you've got two monitors, consider putting the Sidebar on the one that doesn't have your active windows. That way you can always see it.

Tweaking and Changing Gadget Settings

Okay, we're back to gadgets. The way a gadget acts isn't written in stone. For example, how useful would the Clock gadget be if it always showed the time for the West Coast and you lived on the East Coast? Not very. Since everyone wants something different from their gadgets, Vista includes a way to customize them to your needs. Here's how: Look in your Sidebar and find the gadget you'd like to customize. Take the Weather gadget, for example. Chances are you're not from Redmond, Washington (that's where Microsoft's headquarters is located), nor do you care about the weather there, so you'll want to change this to someplace you actually care about. To change the location, Right-click on the gadget itself and choose Options. You'll see a small dialog pop out of the lower-left corner of the gadget showing the options available for this specific gadget. In this case, you'd type in a different location and then click on the little Search icon on the right. Once the location is found, just click OK to close the dialog and change the location for which the Weather gadget will show the weather.

TIP

Each gadget has three little icons in the top-right corner when you hover your cursor over the gadget. The center icon is a wrench. If you're one of the blessed people with super-perfect vision that can actually see that tiny little bugger, then you can click on it to display the Options dialog.

Moving Gadgets

You can move the order in which your gadgets are displayed in the Sidebar. Say you like the Calendar gadget, but really the Weather and Stocks gadgets are more important to you. However, when you look at the Sidebar, for some reason the Calendar gadget appears at the top. No sweat. Just click on the Calendar gadget and drag it downward to the position you'd like. Or click-and-drag the Weather or Stocks gadget upward. Either way, you can move your gadgets around by dragging them into the order that suits you best.

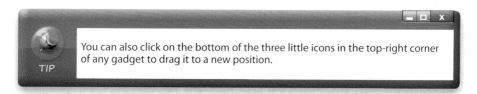

TIP

You can also click on the bottom of the three little icons in the top-right corner of any gadget to drag it to a new position.

Removing Gadgets from the Sidebar

Throughout this chapter we've been talking about gadgets as if they're tied to the Sidebar when, in fact, they're not. I know, it's difficult to hear but it's true. Gadgets are free to roam wherever they want on your desktop. All you need to do is click on one and drag it off of the Sidebar. Move it onto the desktop into an open area and that's where it will stay until you move it again. Let me say this, though, I highly recommend against moving your gadgets out of the Sidebar. The Sidebar is their home by default for a reason. It helps keep things tidy. If it wasn't there, then you'd have gadgets all over the place. It would be anarchy to say the least. Okay, maybe that's an exaggeration (just a bit) but the Sidebar does indeed help keep your gadgets organized and in one place. I suggest you help keep order in the world by leaving them there.

Using the Clock Gadget

The Clock gadget doesn't need much of an introduction. It tells time. There you have it. Not too earth shattering, right? I do like the fact that it's large and stays right in the Sidebar so I can keep track of time. When you click on the gadget options for the clock, you get a few different settings to change. First off you can change the style of clock, which is just a visual change. You can also give the clock a name. Something like "Home" or "Tampa" would work. Next, you can change the Time Zone on the pop-up menu. Finally, you can control whether or not the second hand shows on the clock.

TIP

One way I really get a lot of mileage from the Clock gadget is to have multiple clocks in the Sidebar. If you deal with people from different time zones, then that's a perfect reason to go ahead and drag another clock over to the Sidebar, set it to that time zone, and give it a helpful name.

Using the Notes Gadget

You know those little sticky notes that you (or someone you know) have all over the desk? Well, it's time to take them digital. Forget paper and start putting the information you'd normally write on a sticky note onto a Notes gadget. Some of the options associated with the Notes gadget include the ability to change the color of the note, the font, and the font size. The Notes gadget also has some options when you hover over it. You'll see that as you move your cursor over the gadget, some icons appear. The little plus icon adds another note. After all, who has just one note? You can click the left and right arrows to move between multiple notes. Lastly, you can click on the little X icon to delete the current note. So, say goodbye to paper sticky notes and welcome to the sticky notes of the digital age.

Using the Calendar Gadget

The Calendar gadget is a really easy one to use. It's basically got two views—full month view and single day view. The default view when you add the Calendar gadget is the single day view. If you want to see the current month, then click once on the gadget and it shows the full month view with the current day highlighted. Easy, huh? To switch back to the current day, click on the highlighted day on the full month view (or click on whichever day you want to see in single day view).

Using the Contacts Gadget

The Contacts gadget is perfect for getting to your contacts without actually going through Windows Contacts. When you add the gadget, it shows a list of your contacts (the ones that you have already entered in Windows Contacts). One cool feature is that you can start drafting an email to that contact by clicking on their email address if you've added it when entering the contact info. Just click on the contact's name to get to the information page you see on the right here. Click on the orange tab on the top left to get back your contact list. If you've got a lot of contacts, then it's quite possible you won't see the contact you need onscreen. If that's the case, then type the name in the Search field to find it. Either way, this gadget comes in really handy in place of always keeping your contacts open.

Using the Stocks Gadget

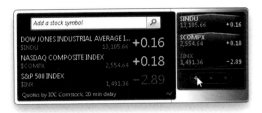

If you own stocks, you know how hard it is to resist checking the latest prices all the time. I know, I know…you're not supposed to check them all the time unless you're day trading. And if you're day trading, then the Stocks gadget probably is pretty lame compared to the software you're using. However, I have to say that I do like to check my stocks a time or two during the day, so I'm going to assume that there's at least one more of you out there (see, as long as there's one of you, then it makes the tip legitimate). Anyway, the Stocks gadget is cool because it keeps your stock prices right in front of you. When things are going good, you'll be able to look over and relish your money-making moments. Luckily, using the gadget is much easier than picking stocks. The first thing you'll want to do is add new stocks to watch. When you hover your cursor over the gadget, you'll see a little plus icon appear. Click it and enter your stock name to add it to the list. Now, if you go into the gadget options, you'll be able to display the stock change as a percentage of the total (instead of the default points) or you can choose to display the full company name instead of just the company's stock symbol. So go ahead. Add your stocks and watch them all day if it makes you happy.

Using the Slide Show Gadget

The Slide Show gadget plays a little slide show over on your Sidebar. It does this auto-matically once you set it up and you really don't need to do anything to change it unless you want to. Personally, while I love slide shows, I find this one a little distracting. I mean, when you're trying to work and you look over and start watching pretty pictures, it really can't be a good thing. That said, it does have a certain cool factor to it. If you want to interact with the gadget, just hover your cursor over it. You'll see a Play/Pause button, which does just what you'd think it does. There's also a Previous button that takes you back a slide and a Next button that takes you forward to the next slide. The button on the far right (with a magnifying glass) will open the current photo in Windows Photo Gallery, where you can start a full-screen slide show. If you go into the Slide Show gadget options, you can change the folder that the gadget will pull photos from. You can also choose how long you want to show each picture, as well as add any cool transitions between the photos when they switch from one to another. All in all, it does have a cool factor.

Using the Currency Gadget

Here's one of my favorites and if you do any international travel, then you'll love this one. The Currency gadget keeps me from having to visit a website to see what my U.S. dollar is worth somewhere else. There aren't any gadget options to change here and nothing really happens when you hover your cursor over it. Basically, what you see is what you get. Here's a good example: Say you're traveling to Europe and the hotel you're looking at staying in costs 100 euros per night. First, click the little down-facing arrow next to the currency name at the top of the gadget (the default is US dollar) and choose the currency type (in this case, euro). Then, type in the amount you want to convert from (100 here) in the field below that currency. Next, choose the currency type that you want to convert to in the bottom half of the gadget (in this case, US dollar). That's it. The gadget does the math for you and tells you the conversion, so you'll know just how much something will cost.

Some of My Favorites

If you're reading this, that means you want to see some of my favorite gadgets. My disclaimer: I have no idea if these are popular or useful for you. That is why the title of the tip is "Some of *My* Favorites." Okay, now that we have that out of the way, let's talk about me. Some of my favorites come with Vista. I love having instant access to my stocks, so the Stocks gadget (top left) is right up there. I love sticky to-do notes (top right), so that is another. They used to be all over my desk, but now they're all over my Sidebar and somehow that makes me feel more organized. Some others that don't come with Vista that I can't do without are My eBay (top center), so I can keep track of my eBay auctions, and App Launcher (bottom center), which lets you shove your favorite programs into a gadget for quick launching, so you don't have to use valuable screen real estate for your Quick Launch toolbar. I also love Package Tracker (bottom left) for tracking my packages without having to visit the carrier website and always typing in a tracking number. Finally, another one that I really like is called Clipboard History (bottom right). It keeps track of the last few clipboard entries (usually for copying-and-pasting) that I made. That way I can always get back to another one with a simple click. Want to know where to get these gadgets and others? Read on to the next tip.

A Popular Gadget Website

If you read the last tip, you're probably wondering where you can get some of those gadgets that don't automatically come with Windows Vista. If you didn't read the last tip, you're probably still asking yourself whether or not there are more gadgets than the few that actually ship with Vista. Well, the good news is that this gadget stuff has actually become a big deal. Large software companies, as well as individual developers, have created tons of free gadgets that are out there for the taking. Here's a great resource for finding just about any type of gadget you can think of: Windows Live Gallery (http://gallery.live.com). Just click on Gadgets in the list on the left, and the Gadgets page will open. Here you can search for a gadget by category in the list on the left, or by keyword using the Search field at the top of the page.

TIP

Be careful here! Downloading gadgets is like eating potato chips—you can never have just one. I know it's a silly analogy, but it's true. First you start off by just trying one new gadget. Next thing you know, it's a week later and you've got 478 new gadgets installed in Vista and nothing else to show for your week's work. While some gadgets are cool, try to keep it to a minimum and just download the ones that you'll use several times a day.

Downloading New Gadgets

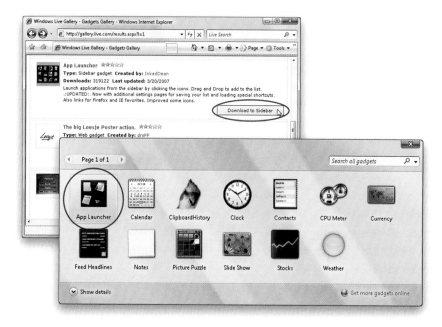

This one is a breeze. Let's say you've gone to the website I mentioned in the previous tip and found a gadget that you really like (App Launcher, in this example). You'll see a button for Download to Sidebar. Click on it and Windows Vista will download a file to your computer. It's usually named somefilename.gadget. Once this file has been downloaded to your computer, just double-click on it to install the gadget. Vista will automatically know that it's a gadget and where it belongs. It will now appear in your Sidebar, and the next time you go to add a new gadget to your Sidebar, you'll see the gadget you just downloaded there—in this case, App Launcher. If you've closed it on your Sidebar, you can just drag it back into your Sidebar, and you're in business.

CHAPTER FOUR

Security!

Keeping Your Computer Safe

Allow? Don't Allow? Continue? Cancel? I've got good news and bad news. Bad news first: get used to seeing the questions at the beginning of this paragraph. The world of online computing has a lot of bad people in it, and they all want to do bad things to your computer, or even retrieve things from your computer and use them against you. Now, for the good news: Vista was made with one main goal in mind—keeping your computer safe. Part of doing that is constantly asking you whether you *really* want to visit a website, install a program, or download something. But there are other parts to keeping secure and safe and they are what we'll look at in this chapter. Yeah, I know it gets kind of annoying, but trust me, in the end your computer will be that much better for it.

Why You Should Worry About Keeping Your Computer Safe

If you've ever had a virus, spyware, or some other unpleasant intrusion into your personal computing life, then you can probably skip this because you already know why it's important. If not, then give it a quick read before moving on. So, here's the deal: every time you turn your computer on and connect to a network or the Internet (wired or wireless), you leave your computer vulnerable to Internet criminals (let's just call them "mean" people) and potentially damaging software (let's just call this "bad" software). Even if you take the highest of precautions for securing your computer, you can still have problems if you share files with other people who haven't taken those precautions. Now, most of what these mean people do and most of their bad software is illegal, but here's the thing—some is not. They have ways of having you agree to download and install programs on your computer that can either invade your privacy or flat-out harm your computer, but that's all done legally. Even if you kept on reading after the first sentence, I'm pretty sure this isn't the first time you've heard of this. This is a huge problem, but Microsoft has been working hard for the past few years to squash this once and for all in Vista. Fortunately, the tools you need are right at your fingertips. It's just up to you to turn them on and leave them on to help protect your computer.

Getting to Everything
Security Related in Vista

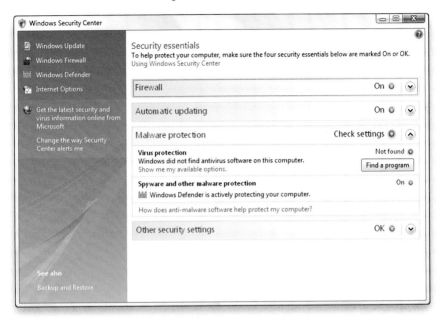

If you're the I-can-figure-it-out-myself kind of person, then this tip is for you. You can find everything security related and get right to it by just going to the Start menu and clicking on Control Panel. Then, look under Security and click on Check This Computer's Security Status. That will open the Windows Security Center. Here's where it all lives, and where you'll find most of what we'll be looking at in this chapter. But, like I said, if you're the I-can-figure-it-out-myself type, then you can get right to it here.

What Spyware and Malware Are and How Your Computer Gets Them

©ISTOCKPHOTO

Spyware is a term given to software that installs itself on a computer and then tracks that computer user's Internet usage. Companies who create this stuff do it mainly for marketing purposes, but it feels like they do it just to annoy the living daylights out of us. Malware stands for malicious software. In fact, it's the new hip term for bad software on computers, and spyware is simply just a category of malware. Malware contains just about every other type of bad software too, though, not just spyware. For example, a virus is also malware (I'll talk more about viruses later in this chapter). Really, it's used to describe any type of software that invades your privacy or deliberately tries to damage your computer or the files and programs on it. Malware can be transmitted through a network, a website on the Internet, emails, CDs and DVDs, downloaded files, and documents you have shared with people you know. This is the stuff you want to protect yourself from because it can either harm the files on your computer or just diminish your personal computing experience and make it annoying.

TIP

One thing to keep in mind is that most malware is not dangerous. Most people out there know not to open files in emails and from people they don't know or trust. Just by doing that, you'll keep most of the damaging stuff off of your computer. Most malware out there is just plain annoying, but it won't go deleting your files or programs so your data is still safe.

Symptoms of Malware on Your Computer

©ISTOCKPHOTO/ LJUPCO SMOKOVSKI

Let's talk about malware first. We'll get into viruses in a few pages. Luckily, it's usually pretty easy to tell if you have any malware on your computer. Here are some symptoms:

- You type in a webpage to visit and another one opens instead.
- Your default homepage is different than the one you specified.
- You see pop-up ads sporadically on your computer, even if you're not surfing the Web.
- When you look at Internet Explorer (or other browsers), you see new toolbars and links that you didn't add.
- In general, your computer seems to run slowly. Plus, you'll also hear your computer processing and churning away even when you're not doing anything.

If you've experienced any of these, chances are you may have some type of malware. No need to freak out though, most malware isn't dangerous to your computer. It's more annoying than anything, but read on and you'll find out how to get rid of it.

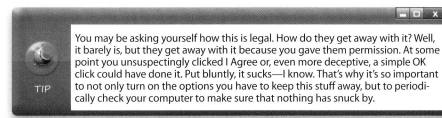

TIP

You may be asking yourself how this is legal. How do they get away with it? Well, it barely is, but they get away with it because you gave them permission. At some point you unsuspectingly clicked I Agree or, even more deceptive, a simple OK click could have done it. Put bluntly, it sucks—I know. That's why it's so important to not only turn on the options you have to keep this stuff away, but to periodically check your computer to make sure that nothing has snuck by.

Getting Rid of and Keeping Malware Off Your Computer

All of this malicious software talk is a little bit scary and probably has you wondering how to detect it and help keep it off your computer. Vista, by default, has a program called Windows Defender that does just that. Windows Defender is a free program that helps detect spyware and similar software on your computer (notice I didn't say viruses, though). You can use it in two ways: First, you can use it to monitor your computer in real-time while you use it. It'll alert you if any bad software tries to install itself and help you keep malware off your computer by deleting it before it even gets on there. Next, you can use Windows Defender to automatically run a scan of your computer every so often (you choose how often) to make sure that no bad software has made its way onto your hard drive. You can get to Windows Defender by going to the Start menu, to All Programs, and choosing Windows Defender. Keep one thing in mind though, and it's probably the most important part of this tip: Windows Defender is *not* antivirus software—it's an anti-spyware program, but will not detect or remove viruses (there are several tips later in this chapter with more info on viruses).

Windows Defender

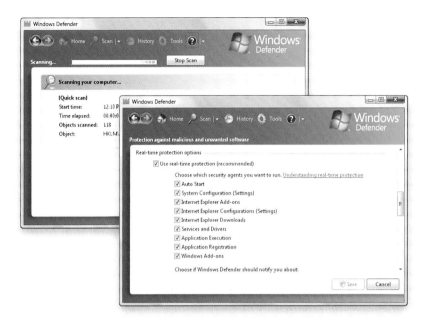

Now let's take a look at how to use Windows Defender. First, open it by going to the Start menu and choosing All Programs>Windows Defender. If you recall from the previous tip, there are two ways to use Windows Defender. The first is to scan your computer for any harmful software that may already be on it. To do that, just press the Scan button and Vista will do the rest. Next, you can also use Windows Defender to protect your computer in real-time in hopes of avoiding the bad software ever even getting onto your computer. To use this part you'll need to make sure that real-time protection is turned on. Click on the Tools button in Windows Defender and, under Settings, choose Options. Scroll down the options window to Real-Time Protection Options. Here you'll need to make sure the Use Real-Time Protection checkbox is turned on. That way, Vista will help protect your computer as you work, to avoid having any bad software make it onto your system.

What to Do If You Suspect Malware
But Can't Get a Pop-Up to Close

First things first: Don't click OK. Don't click I Accept, Yes, or whatever other affirming message appears. Sometimes you'll get caught in this endless loop of windows that won't close without you agreeing to install some type of malware. If that happens, you can try a few things, but don't be shy about going to the last resort right away. First, forget about trying to close all of the windows. Cut straight to it and Right-click on the Internet Explorer 7 (or other browser) window icon in the Taskbar and choose Close (or just press Alt-F4). If that doesn't work, then I suggest rebooting altogether. Make sure you switch to any programs with open and unsaved work and save it. Then reboot and don't visit that site again.

What Is a Virus and How Is It Different from Spyware?

A virus is a different form of malware because it can be destructive (FYI: You may also have heard viruses referred to as worms or Trojan horses). While spyware can be destructive from the aspect of slowing down your computer and lessening your enjoyment of your Internet experience, a virus can be destructive to the point of destroying your important files. Here's the really important part, though: not only is a virus different, but the way that Vista handles them is different. You see, Vista includes ways to protect your computer from spyware. However, it doesn't include any type of virus protection. This means that, out of the box, Vista will not protect your computer from viruses you can get from emailing or downloading files. If you want to get virus protection, you're going to need some type of third-party software for that.

Protecting Your Computer from Viruses

There are a few ways to protect your computer from a virus and different degrees of protection. First, there is the software method, which consists of three steps: (a) You need to install third-party antivirus software. These programs will scan your incoming and outgoing emails and periodically scan your files for viruses. New viruses are created every day, so make sure you have it check for updates often. Next, (b) turn on Automatic Updating in Vista (covered later in this chapter). This alone will protect you from many of the threats out there. Then, (c) turn on Windows Firewall (also covered later). This will prevent those "mean" people from gaining unauthorized access to your computer and installing a virus without you knowing. The other ways to protect your computer from a virus are not software-related, they're user-related—and by user, I mean you. Do not open attachments from email addresses that you don't know or trust. Don't download files from websites that you don't trust or Internet sharing websites, where you might as well make your screen name "I love viruses and please give them to me" if you're going to use them. They're packed full of software that will wreak havoc on your computer, which they're counting on you to download and install.

TIP

To find trusted, Vista-compatible, antivirus software, you can visit Microsoft's Antivirus Partners website by clicking the Find a Program button under Malware Protection in the Windows Security Center.

Determining If You Have a Virus

If you've read any of the previous tips about viruses, then you already know Vista doesn't come with antivirus software. Out of the box, there's no way for Vista to tell if you have a virus let alone get rid of that virus for you. That's why you need some type of third-party antivirus software as mentioned in the earlier tips. These programs not only monitor your computer for viruses, but they can remove them if you already have one. There are quite a few companies that provide antivirus software at a reasonable price for Windows, but here are some good recommendations (all of which provide free trial downloads):

- Windows Live One Care (http://onecare.live.com)
- Symantec (www.symantec.com)
- McAfee (www.mcafee.com)

The Importance of Automatic Updates

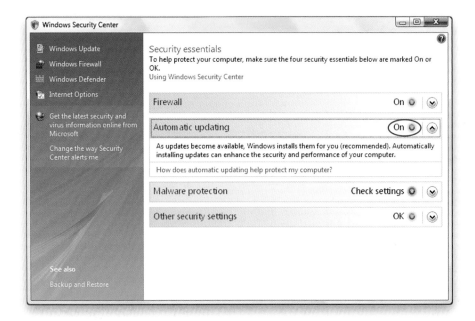

Automatic updates are one of the main ways you can protect your computer. Let me lay it out for you. Wouldn't it be great if Microsoft developed an operating system that automatically and unequivocally protected your computer from every potential threat or virus out there forever? Sure it would. But that is not the reality. The reality is that when they built Windows Vista it did protect against any threats that were known at the time. However, the human spirit is one heck of a resilient one. If at first you don't succeed, then try again, right? Well that is how software hackers operate. There are those geeky genius kids or adults who have nothing better to do with their time than sit in front of their computers and develop ways to harm other computers. As they come up with new ways to exploit your operating system or the software on it, Microsoft creates fixes and updates to help thwart those exploits. That's where turning on Automatic Updating comes in. Over the years, we've all heard the horror stories about computers from large companies being hacked into and exploited in some way. Well, most of those attacks have happened because the computers were not kept up-to-date. In fact, in very few circumstances did an attack result from a brand spanking new vulnerability that Windows didn't already have an update ready for. The problem has been that people just didn't install the update to close that vulnerability. So it's vital to turn Automatic Updating on and leave it on. Let the tools that are already in Vista to help protect you do their job.

Turning On Automatic Updating

You can turn on Automatic Updating in the Windows Security Center. Just go to the Start menu and click on Control Panel. Under Security, choose Check This Computer's Security Status. Just below the Firewall option is Automatic Updating. If the area around the text is red, that means Automatic Updating is totally off. If it's amber, it means you have enabled some features of Automatic Updating but you're not taking advantage of all of them. If it's green, you can just stop here because Automatic Updating is already on and your job is done. So, if it's red or amber, click on Windows Update at the top left of the window. In the resulting window, click on Change Settings on the left. Here, you'll be asked if you want to Install Updates Automatically, if you'd like to choose the updates that are downloaded and installed, or if you want Vista to Never Check for Updates. I suggest clicking the Install Updates Automatically radio button. That way your updates are downloaded and installed automatically and your computer will be kept safer without you having to do a thing.

TIP

By default, automatic updates are set to be installed every day at 3:00 a.m. If your computer is not on, then the updates can't be installed. If you're using your computer at that time, you may notice it slows down a bit while updating (you've got bigger problems if you're up every night at 3:00 a.m.). If either of these becomes a long-term problem, go to the Change Settings window and change the time setting to whatever works best for you.

What Is Windows Firewall?

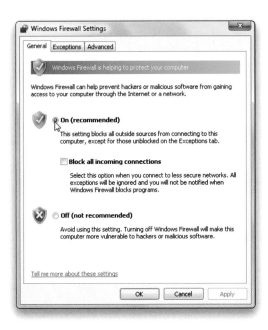

As we talked about earlier, there are lots of ways that viruses and unwanted software can get installed on your computer. Usually, it involves you running a program or opening an attachment that you shouldn't have. However, it doesn't always work that way. Sometimes, people can gain unauthorized access to your computer through a network or the Internet and install something on your computer without you ever knowing. That's where Windows Firewall comes in. A firewall is software that scans all incoming information from a network or the Internet and decides what is safe and what is not. If it decides someone trying to connect to your computer is not safe and could possibly harm your computer, then the firewall will block them. Windows Vista comes with a firewall program, and all you really have to do is make sure you keep it on. To do this, go to the Security window (Start>Control Panel>Security) and look under Windows Firewall. Click the link that reads Turn Windows Firewall On or Off, and the Windows Firewall Settings dialog will open. Here, just make sure that the On radio button is turned on. If not, then click on it and click OK.

Why You Should Back Up Your Computer

©ISTOCKPHOTO/EMRAH TURUDU

True story. As I sit here and write this tip, I'm thinking of a conversation I had yesterday with my buddy Steve. See, Steve was telling me his hard drive started making this weird noise, and then his computer wouldn't boot anymore. While I'm not a computer technician, I've had this happen enough times to me (about three times in the last five years) to know that it's the sure sign of a hard drive crash. So, I asked if he had a backup. As you can imagine, I wouldn't be telling this story if he said yes. Steve didn't have a backup. I asked him why and he said, "I just never thought it was going to happen to me." He knew that it had happened to a lot of other people, but for some reason he thought he was immune to a hard drive failure. Here's the thing: it's not *if* your hard drive fails, it's a matter of *when* your hard drive fails. At some point, you will be affected by the loss of your precious computer files. These files probably have your financial information in them, important work information, addresses and email messages, and your family photos, which are irreplaceable. So make sure you read the rest of this chapter to help minimize the damage.

Backing Up the Files on Your Computer

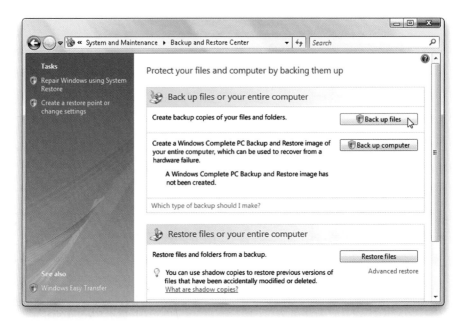

In Vista, backups are a breeze. Just go to the Control Panel (from the Start menu) and look under System and Maintenance. Click the Back Up Your Computer link to open the Backup and Restore Center. In here you have two backup options: (1) backing up the files and folders on your computer, and (2) creating a Windows Complete PC Backup and Restore image (not available in Home Basic; see the next tip). The difference between the two is pretty simple: Backing up the files and folders (by clicking the Back Up Files button) makes exact copies of all the files on your computer. With that backup, you could either restore the files in case of a crash or even move them to another computer. Plus, you have access on that backup to each and every individual file, so you can pick and choose which ones you want to restore later. Option (2) is best suited for creating a complete disk image of your computer when it's in a happy place, say when you first install Windows and all of your programs. An image is basically a snapshot of your computer's installed programs, files, and folder structure all lumped into one file. That way, should anything ever happen to your hard drive, you can restore that image and your computer will be taken back to that very point. You would not use this option to create backups of the files and folders on your computer, though. Option (1) is better for this. So my suggestion is this: after you install Vista (or buy a new computer), go ahead and use option (2) to make a full system backup. Now you've got a good restore point should anything happen. Then use option (1) periodically to create backups of the files on your computer, so you know the actual data you need is safe and you can always load the files if they're ever needed.

Backing Up Your Entire Computer

If you remember from the last tip, this option is good for making a copy of your entire computer system. A good time to do this is when you first get your computer running with Vista and all of the programs you use installed on it. It's also good to run this every now and then after you've installed new programs. This saves a lot of time should your hard drive ever crash. You won't need to go back and reinstall everything. To back up the entire computer using the Windows Complete PC Backup and Restore image, go to the Control Panel (from the Start menu) and look under System and Maintenance. Click the Back Up Your Computer link to go into the Backup and Restore Center. Under the Back Up Files or Your Entire Computer section, click the Back Up Computer button. This walks you through the wizard to create an entire backup of your computer. The first step is to choose where you want to store your backup. Choose a location and then click Next. The next screen confirms your settings. If you're happy with them, then click the Start Backup button and you're in business.

Where to Store Backups

Where you store your backups is almost as important as backing up itself. If you leave with any one piece of advice from this tip, I hope it's this: do *not* store your backup on the same hard drive that Windows runs on. Why? Because if your computer hard drive ever crashes, then your backup is gone along with everything else. There are really only two good options for backups: one is a DVD and the other is an external hard drive. Me personally, I use both because each has pros and cons. DVDs are great. They're easy to store offsite and pretty cheap to purchase. But you may misplace them, or scratch them, or do something that could cause them to become unreadable. An external hard drive is like your computer hard drive, but it's not in your computer—it's a separate device that you connect (usually through a USB cable). These work great, too. However, they are, after all, electronic and governed by all of the rules and regulations that electronics typically face (read as: they can sometimes stop working for no reason at all). So my preference is to use both. I create a backup to an external hard drive. Then I copy that to a DVD, so now I have two backups and that should keep me fairly safe in case my hard drive ever does crash.

It's also a good idea to store one of your backups offsite every once in a while. You never know what catastrophe may strike, and if your data is important to you, then it's good to keep one at a friend's or family member's house just in case.

Restoring Your Computer from a Backup

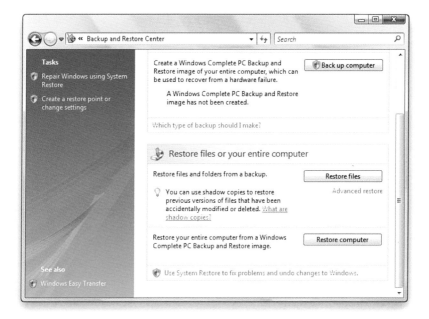

Regardless of which backup option you chose, restoring your backup is probably even easier. Go into the Backup and Restore Center (which is where you went to back up the computer in the first place—Start>Control Panel>Back Up Your Computer) and look toward the bottom of the window. There you'll see Restore Files or Your Entire Computer. At this point, you'll need to know which type of backup you made and you'll need the actual backup copy (which is probably on a CD, DVD, or external hard drive). Then click either Restore Files, if you chose the Back Up Files option before, or Restore Computer, if you chose the Back Up Computer option before. Either way, Vista walks you through the process of restoring the backup.

Automatically Backing Up Your Computer

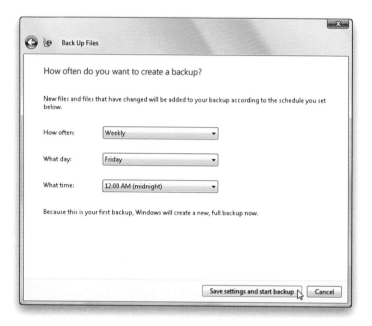

Automatically backing up your computer is actually one of the settings you go through when you're backing the computer up in the first place. Go into the Backup and Restore Center (Start>Control Panel>Back Up Your Computer) and click the Back Up Files button. Once you choose where to back up to, click Next. Then choose which file types you want to back up. The last screen will prompt you to choose how often you want to create a backup. Choose the settings here (or change them if you've already chosen them before) and click Save Settings and Start Backup. I suggest at least a weekly backup schedule. I find Friday nights work well for me, and I'll choose a time that is in the middle of the night so I'm less likely to be on the computer.

You may have heard about Vista Service Pack 1, also called SP1, for short. Essentially, SP1 is a cumulative collection of all fixes that have been released for Vista since it first came out. This includes performance enhancements, compatibility fixes, and most importantly, security updates. Think of it like a band's greatest hits collection—it's not anything new, it's just all of the best stuff wrapped up in one place. Depending on when you're reading this and when you got your computer (or upgraded to Vista), you may or may not already have SP1 (see the tip below to find out how to tell if you do or don't). If you don't, then you should definitely install it. Another question that's just as important is, "What is SP1 *not*?" It's not new stuff. You're not going to actually see any of the changes in the user interface or any new programs. It's all under-the-hood stuff to make your computer run better. So, even if you think you've kept current with all of your updates, make sure you install SP1, because there are always a few new things thrown in the actual service pack that make it worth installing.

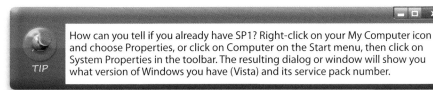

How can you tell if you already have SP1? Right-click on your My Computer icon and choose Properties, or click on Computer on the Start menu, then click on System Properties in the toolbar. The resulting dialog or window will show you what version of Windows you have (Vista) and its service pack number.

How Do I Get SP1?

There are three ways to get SP1. But, before you try to get it, make sure you don't already have it installed on your computer. You may, and may not even know it. The tip at the bottom of the previous page tells you how to check. Now, on to how to get SP1:

1. The first method is called Express, and you can do it through the Windows Update once SP1 is publicly available. The only real downside to this method is that it takes a while. You'll need a decent Internet connection to be able to download the service pack, which is kind of big, so if you don't have a cable modem or better, you may want to stay clear of this one. You can always give it a try, and if your estimated download time says 38 hours, then maybe try another way.

2. The next method is called stand-alone. This means the service pack comes as one big file. If you have a few computers in your house, then you may want to consider this one over the others, because you can always burn the file to a CD and quickly put it onto other computers, as well. You can usually get the stand-alone version in one of two ways: (a) download it from Microsoft's website, or (b) I've seen Microsoft distribute free CDs with the service pack on them (they did this with XP).

3. The last way is through the Vista install disc. After the service pack is officially released, Microsoft includes SP1 on the actual Vista install disc. So, if you buy Vista from a store after SP1's release, chances are it'll have SP1 on it. One way to check is to look at the box or on the disc label, and it'll tell you whether it has SP1.

Once you have it, then you need to install it. We'll look at that on the next page.

How Do I Install SP1?

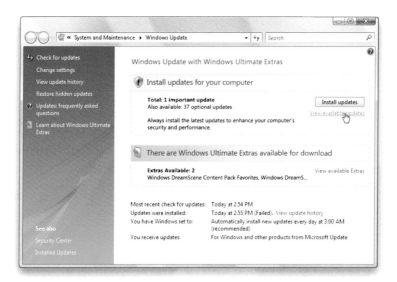

Okay, you have (or at least you know how to get) SP1. Now you have to install it.

Step 1: Regardless of which method you use, I suggest you do an entire system backup. This is a fairly major upgrade and you want to make sure you have all of your personal files backed up (emails, documents, photos, etc.). You can read more about backups earlier in this chapter. This is also a good time to get rid of any programs you don't use through Add/Remove Programs. The less junk you have on your system, the better.

Step 2: Now that things are backed up, you can start the install. If you're going the on-line route through Windows Update, go to the Control Panel and, under Security, click on Check for Updates. If SP1 is available, it'll show up as a pending update. Click on View Available Updates to see the list of available updates. If you've downloaded the single file or have SP1 on a disc, go ahead and launch the installer file to start the process.

Step 3: Wait. Then wait some more. This part is slow, and can keep you from using your computer for an hour (or more). Now is a good time to brush up on your *Guitar Hero* skills or catch up on some old episodes of *Lost*. And, hey, if *American Idol* is your thing well…you know who you are.

TIP I probably don't need to say this, but…make sure your computer is plugged in and the power is not interrupted during the install. Sounds like a no-brainer, but if you've got a laptop, plug it in. Also, you probably don't want to try this during a lightning storm when power outages can happen. Hey, I'm just sayin'….

CHAPTER FIVE

Surfing the Web
Getting Online Quickly & Safely

When most people are asked why they bought a computer, one of their top answers is always "to surf the Web." Well, surfing just got better in Vista. With the introduction of Internet Explorer 7 (IE7), you're going to find that the Web experience is a lot more enjoyable. Some of the things we'll look at in this chapter are: getting your computer on the Web, and all of the new features in IE7 to try out once you're there. You'll see how to use the brand new Tabs feature (the coolest feature, in my book), download files, keep track of your favorite blogs, search the Web more easily, and even how to use add-ons for IE7.

Quickly Connect to a Wireless Network

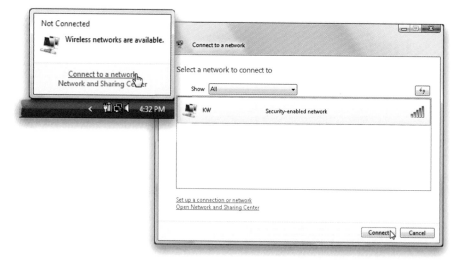

If all you want to do is connect to a wireless network (say you're on a laptop in an airport or coffee shop), then there is a quick way to do it. Once you start Windows Vista, look in the notification area of the Taskbar (the little icon area at the bottom right of the screen). In there, you should see a little icon with two computers and an X through it, if you're not already connected to a network. Click that icon and a small pop-up window will open above it. Click the Connect to a Network link and it'll open the Connect to a Network dialog. You'll see a list of available wireless networks. Click on the wireless network that you want to connect to, and then click Connect. Keep in mind that you'll need a security code or password for any wireless networks that have Security-Enabled Network showing next to their name. If you don't have that password, then you won't be able to connect to it.

Your Internet and Networking Home

Vista has the new Network and Sharing Center that takes care of everything you need to connect to the Internet or another network. To get to it, go to the Start menu and click on Control Panel. When the Control Panel opens, choose Network and Internet. Then go ahead and click on the very top listing called Network and Sharing Center. This is essentially your one-stop shop for everything you need to connect to the Internet. When you look at the window (if you're connected to a network), you'll see it's broken up into four areas: The top is the status area, and it gives you a visual map of what your connection looks like. The next area shows you the details of the network you're connected to, including the name, whether it's private or public, and whether or not you have Internet access through that network. In my window, you can see for Access it reads Local and Internet. That means that I can work with other computers attached to my network, as well as access the Internet. Next you have the Sharing and Discovery section, which shows you what type of detection settings you have on (whether your computer will automatically look for a network or wait for you to do it) and what type of sharing options are turned on (Printer, File, Media, etc.). The last section is on the left side of the window, and it's all of the tasks that you'd typically want to do when it comes to connecting to the Internet and networking. So, think of this window as your little networking home base. Whenever you need to connect to another computer, network, or the Internet, this is where you'll come.

How to Know If You're Currently Connected to the Internet

If you're not sure whether you're connected to the Internet, then go to the Network and Sharing Center (Start>Control Panel>Network and Internet>Network and Sharing Center). If you're not connected to the Internet, you'll see a few indicators:

1 The network map diagram at the top of the window will show a red X through the connection line between your computer and the Internet icon.

2 The status area right under the connection diagram will read Not Connected.

3 Your Connection icon in the notification area of the Taskbar will have a little red X on it.

If you're connected to the Internet, then you won't see any of the three items mentioned above. In fact, you shouldn't see any red X's in your network map diagram or on the Connection icon in the notification area, and instead of seeing Not Connected in the status area, you'll see the name of your network. I'll talk about connecting to the Internet or a network on the next few pages.

Connecting to an Existing Internet Connection

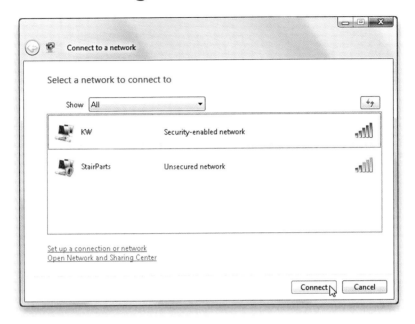

If you plug your computer into a broadband or wireless network that already exists, then this tip is for you. First, go to the Network and Sharing Center (Start>Control Panel> Network and Internet>Network and Sharing Center). In the Tasks section on the left, click on the Connect to a Network link. That'll open a dialog listing all of your available network and Internet connections. Click on the name of your network to connect to it and then click the Connect button at the bottom of the dialog. If you're successful in connecting to the network, you'll see a window that says you're successfully connected to your network. It also shows you a little checkbox that asks if you'd like to save this network. Saving the network makes it easier to connect next time, and Vista can do it automatically if you'd like, so go ahead and turn that option on. Then click the Close button and you're in business.

TIP

As you can imagine, in Vista there are always multiple ways to do things. If you need to quickly connect to a network or view your current connection, you can click on the Connection icon in the notification area of your Taskbar and choose Connect to a Network or choose Connect To from the Start menu.

Setting Up an Internet Connection

Okay, before we get too far, make sure you have an Internet connection (DSL, cable modem, or dial-up). Then make sure it's connected to your computer (if it's not wireless). Now go to the Network and Sharing Center (Start>Control Panel>Network and Internet> Network and Sharing Center). In the Tasks area, click on Set Up a Connection or Network. This window gives you options for the kind of network you want to create. Here, you'll want to worry about connecting to the Internet, so choose Connect to the Internet and click Next. The next window (shown above) asks which type of connection you're using. Your choices are Wireless, Broadband (PPPoE), and Dial-Up, so click on the option you're using. If you choose Wireless, Vista will open a window showing you which wireless networks are available. If you choose Broadband, the next window will ask you for the connection information your ISP provided you. The last option, Dial-Up, will ask you for the phone number, user name, and password required to connect. If you're choosing Wireless, just select the network you're connecting to and click Connect. In the other two options, fill in the required information and click Connect to create the new connection.

TIP

If you already know you have an Internet connection (cable modem, dial-up, or DSL) then skip this tip. If you don't, then make sure you get one before you try to connect to the Internet. Your best bet is to call your local cable or phone company, as they usually offer reasonably priced, fast Internet connections for their subscribers.

Sharing Your Files or Printers with Other Computers

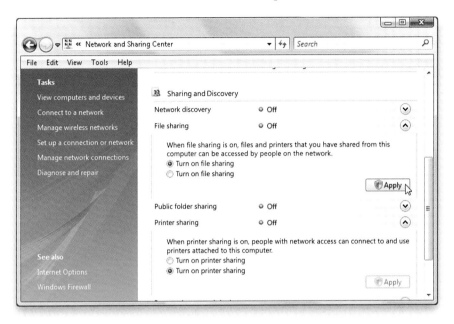

Most homes, and definitely most offices, have multiple computers in them. Even if your home doesn't have multiple computers, chances are you have more than one person using your computer. One of the things that will undoubtedly make things easier is if you can share files and printers between those computers. That way, your husband, wife, kids, or co-workers have an easy way to see files or printers that you're using without you having to burn them to a disc or transfer them to another drive. So here's how to turn this on: Go to the Network and Sharing Center (Start>Control Panel>Network and Internet>Network and Sharing Center). You'll see the Sharing and Discovery section at the bottom of the window. If you don't, that probably means you're not connected to a network, so you'll need to do that first. Then, under Sharing and Discovery, you'll see a few options that we can use here—the first is File Sharing. If you click on the Off radio button, the option will expand and give you a brief description of what you can do here. If you turn this option on, then people on your network can access any files you have shared. Another option below File Sharing is Printer Sharing. This one works the same way. If you turn it on, then anyone with access to your network can use printers that are attached to your computer. This works great if your husband or wife has a computer and printer in their office and you have one in, say, the kitchen. Who wants to have two printers sitting around? Just connect the printer to one computer and share it. That way, the other person can use the same printer.

What Public Folders Are and How to Share Them

Public folders are a built-in way for Vista to keep track of the files you want to share. They're categorized into folders of the most common types of files that people share—documents, downloads, music, pictures, and videos. They're a great way to share files between people on your network without going through any hassle. They do require you to do two things before you share: first, you need to enable sharing, and then you need to put files into those folders. To do this, go to the Network and Sharing Center (Start>Control Panel>Network and Internet>Network and Sharing Center). You'll see the Sharing and Discovery section at the bottom of the window. Click on the down-facing arrow next to Public Folder Sharing to expand that section. Then, click on the radio button for either Turn On option based on what you want to let other people do. You can let them simply view the files or you can let them view and change the files in the public folders. After that, the only thing left is to place files into those folders so others have something to see.

Getting the Latest
Internet Explorer Web Browser

Okay…you got me. This is actually a trick title. You really don't need to do anything to get the latest Web browser (affectionately known as IE7). It comes with Vista, so by installing Vista you have already installed IE7. Why is this big news? For starters, as Windows users we haven't gotten a new Web browser for years until IE7's recent release. Internet Explorer 6 did a lot of good things, but let's face it—it was old. IE7 steps in as the new kid on the block and will quickly take the reins as most popular browser. It takes Internet browsing to a whole new level. For starters, it looks brand new and it takes a lot of the clutter away from the Web browser, so the area you view your webpages in is maximized when it comes to space. It's also got tabbed browsing, which is a new way to surf multiple websites at the same time without cluttering up your desktop with a bunch of windows. Throw in improved searching, printing, and the ability to view and organize your RSS feeds right within the browser, and you've got one sweet new Web browser.

Getting Familiar with Tabbed Surfing

Picture this: you're sitting at your computer and you open a Web browser to check the latest news. If you're like me, you have ADSD. That's short for Attention Deficit Surfing Disorder. It's actually a very widespread epidemic and the CDC is investigating it now. Because of your ADSD, you can't finish reading the news before the urge to check your stocks emerges. However, you also have a commitment phobia (wow, you've got problems), so you don't want to commit to the stock site and close the news window down. So what do you do? Just open another Web browser window. Now you've got two. While you're looking at stocks, you decide to check out your auction on eBay and, sadly, you know what happens next. Yep, you open yet another Web browser window. Aside from the fact that you need some serious help with all of your disorders and things, you also need what is called tabbed browsing. Tabs let you open multiple websites within one browser window. They're a lifesaver, and now that I've used them I don't think I could ever go back.

How Tabbed Surfing Works

Tabbed surfing is a breeze. The way it works is this: Launch Internet Explorer 7 by going under the Start menu or clicking on the IE7 icon in your Quick Launch toolbar. Type in a Web address to visit a site. If you look toward the top of the window right next to the two little Favorites stars, you'll see a tab that shows the site you're visiting. Right next to it you'll see a blank tab. Just click that tab to open a new blank one, then type in another Web address to visit another site. Again, press the little blank tab button to the right of the new tab to open another tab and do the same thing. Now you've got three sites open in one browser window. It's much easier to keep track of your tabbed windows and it makes surfing multiple sites at the same time a breeze. To switch back to another tab, just click once on it in the tab area and you'll see that site just as you left it. If you haven't guessed yet, I love tabs. I'm telling ya though—they're addictive, so be careful.

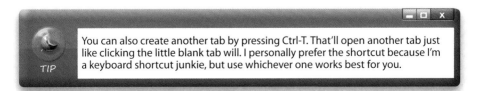

TIP

You can also create another tab by pressing Ctrl-T. That'll open another tab just like clicking the little blank tab will. I personally prefer the shortcut because I'm a keyboard shortcut junkie, but use whichever one works best for you.

Opening Multiple Tabs
When You Open IE7

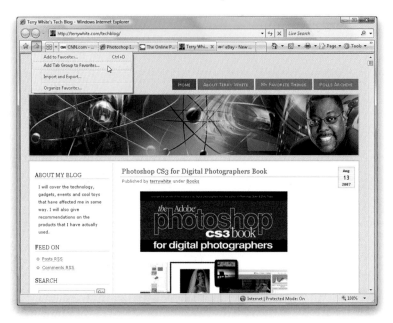

Here's my typical surf routine in the morning: First I check the news at CNN.com. That's one tab. Then I have a few favorite industry news sites (I'm in the digital imaging industry), so I visit a few blogs right off the bat—Scott Kelby's *Adobe Photoshop Insider* (www.scottkelby .com), *The Online Photographer* (http://theonlinephotographer.com), and *Terry White's Tech Blog* (http://terrywhite.com/techblog/). There are four tabs in total. I'm an eBay fan and there's always an auction that I'm watching, so I check that site out, and that makes five tabs. By now you get the picture, right? I do this every day, so why go through the hassle of opening these sites each time I start out my day? Well, you don't have to with Internet Explorer 7 because there's something called a tab group. This is an easy way to save a group of tabs as a favorite, just as you would save an individual site. To use them, just open all of the webpages that you want to save as a group. Then click the Add to Favorites button at the top-left corner of IE7 (it's the yellow star with the plus icon in it, or just press Alt-Z). Then choose Add Tab Group to Favorites from the menu that pops up. Give your tab group a descriptive name (like "My Daily Sites") and click Add. Then, you can close IE7 anytime. When you reopen it, just go to your Favorites menu (the little yellow star icon) and the group you just saved will appear as a folder in the list of favorites. Just put your cursor over that folder and click the little right-facing arrow to the right of the group name to reopen all of those tabs automatically. Have I mentioned that I really love tabs?

Don't Type the Whole Address

This actually isn't anything new in Vista, but I thought it was a cool tip. You know how everyone is used to typing www, dot, and then whatever URL they want to get to? Then they always follow it up with a dot com. Well, you don't always need the www dot. For example, if you wanted to visit Yahoo's website, just type yahoo.com and hit Enter. It's the same thing as typing it the long way. Cool, huh? It's not perfect, so sometimes you may have to add the www. But for most websites it works just fine—just give it a try.

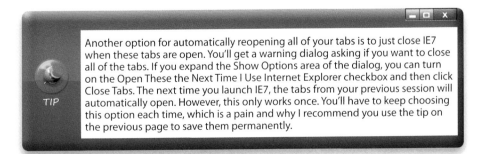

TIP

Another option for automatically reopening all of your tabs is to just close IE7 when these tabs are open. You'll get a warning dialog asking if you want to close all of the tabs. If you expand the Show Options area of the dialog, you can turn on the Open These the Next Time I Use Internet Explorer checkbox and then click Close Tabs. The next time you launch IE7, the tabs from your previous session will automatically open. However, this only works once. You'll have to keep choosing this option each time, which is a pain and why I recommend you use the tip on the previous page to save them permanently.

Favorites

Internet Explorer 7 has a new Favorites Center that localizes the three things you'll want to get to most in your Web browser: website favorites, RSS feeds, and your browser history. To get to it press the small yellow star button at the left end of the browser toolbar (you can also press Alt-C to open it). This opens the Favorites Center in a panel on the left side of the window. At the top of the Favorites Center, you'll see a Favorites button that holds all of the favorite webpage addresses you save. Then you'll see a Feeds button. If you press that, you'll see all of the RSS feeds that you have saved. Finally, the last one is the History button. This shows you your recent browser history, so if you know you went to a website recently but can't remember the address, give the history a try. I've actually grown very accustomed to having the Favorites Center open all of the time, too. If screen real estate isn't a problem and you've got enough screen to make it feasible, keeping the Favorites Center open makes it that much easier to get to the things you use most.

Searching the Web from IE7

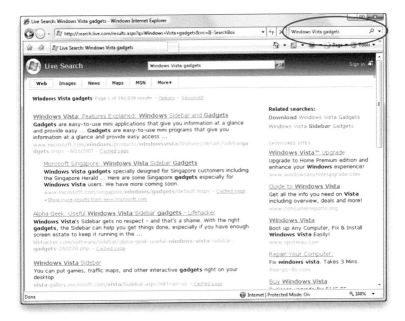

Searching the Web also got easier with Internet Explorer 7. Now, everything you need to search with is right in your main window. To search the Web, click in the search field in the top-right corner of IE7 and type in your search terms (by default, IE7 uses Live Search). Press Enter to search for websites and results that match those terms. IE7 will think for a moment and then show you a list of sites that meet the criteria. Then, just click a link to follow it to the original website.

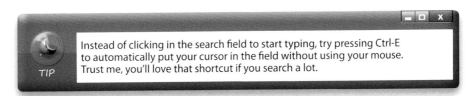

Instead of clicking in the search field to start typing, try pressing Ctrl-E to automatically put your cursor in the field without using your mouse. Trust me, you'll love that shortcut if you search a lot.

TIP

Using Other Search Engines

Everyone has a favorite search engine on the Web. For some it's Google, for others it's Yahoo, and for others it may be Lycos. Internet Explorer 7 brings all of those search engines to you so you don't have to visit multiple sites and open multiple windows or pages. For example, by default IE7 uses Microsoft's search engine, Live Search, to search the Web. However, Google is another popular search engine. Well, you can perform a Google search, just like you did with Live Search in the previous tip, right within IE7, but you need to add a new search provider first. To do this, just click the down-facing arrow next to the search field and choose Find More Providers. You'll see a new page that displays various Web and topic searches (you can even choose to search eBay). One of the Web Search options is Google. Click on it and the Add Search Provider dialog will open. You can just click the Add Provider button to add Google as another search provider. However, if you want to make it your default search engine, make sure you turn on the checkbox to do so. Now when you go to search the Web, you can use Google by clicking the down-facing arrow again and choosing it from the search field's pop-up menu (if you didn't specify it as the default) or you'll know you're already using it because your search field will show "Google" in light gray text when no text has been entered. Now, just search like you normally would and your results will be based on the search provider you chose instead of Live Search. Even better, you can add multiple search providers like this, and they'll all appear in the search field's pop-up menu.

Printing Your Webpages

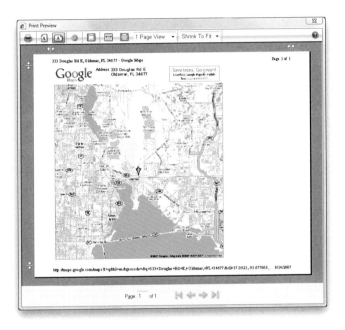

If you ever printed a webpage before Internet Explorer 7 and it didn't look like what you saw on the screen, then this tip is for you. In IE7, there's improved webpage printing so the page that you see onscreen fits on the page that you print. IE7 will automatically shrink the text so it all fits on the printed page the way you saw it onscreen. You can also customize the margins, layout, and even remove the headers and footers from the page. To do this, go to a website just as you normally would. Then go to the toolbar and click the Print button. That'll print the page to your default printer. If, instead, you click on the down-facing arrow next to the Print button and choose Print, it'll open the Print dialog where you can specify the printer you want to print to, as well as other print options. Alternatively, if you want to see what your webpage will look like on paper before printing, then click the down-facing arrow next to the Print button and choose Print Preview. There, you can choose portrait or landscape printing (do you want the page long or wide?), as well as preview what the page will look like on paper. When you're ready, just press the Print button (the printer icon) in the top-left corner.

Downloading Files from the Internet

Surfing the Web is practically synonymous with downloading files. Internet Explorer 7 has a default download folder and I suggest just leaving it the way it is. I used to create my own folder, but after years of using custom folders, I've realized that using the folders Windows suggests is the best way to go. So, when you go to a website and download a file, you'll see the dialog on the left above. You have the option to just run (or open) the file (it won't be saved anywhere), or the option to save it to your computer. I typically choose the latter, so just click Save. The Save As dialog will open asking you where on your computer you want to save the file. Unless you've changed it, the Downloads folder is the default folder, but you can verify that by looking at the folder location at the top of the dialog. Notice that mine says mattk>Downloads. If it isn't the default folder, you can save it there anyway by going to the left side of the dialog and choosing Downloads under your username in the Folders section. Just remember where you save that download, so once it's time to use it you can get to it.

Blocking Pop-Up Ads

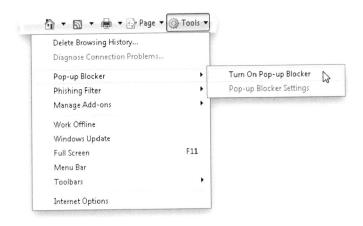

Have you ever visited a website, caught a quick glimpse of the homepage, and then had three or four windows pop up on you trying to sell you everything from Viagra to a certified online degree (and you can get it in only three minutes)? Well, my privacy-invaded friends, those are called pop-ups. Luckily, Internet Explorer 7 comes with a pop-up blocker built right in to help block those annoying ads. It will typically be on by default, but you can verify or turn it on and off by clicking on the Tools button in IE7's toolbar and choosing Pop-Up Blocker>Turn On (or Off, if you'd like) Pop-Up Blocker. My suggestion is to always leave that sucker on because there is rarely a time when you want pop-up ads.

Changing Pop-Up Blocker Settings

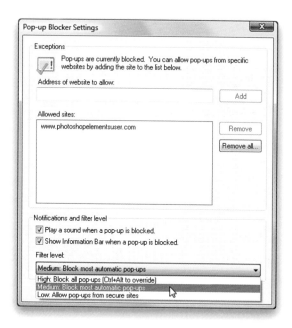

If you find that the built-in pop-up blocker is letting too many pop-up ads through or is blocking too many pop-ups (ones you want, such as a login page), then try this: Click on the Tools button in the toolbar and choose Pop-Up Blocker>Pop-Up Blocker Settings. Here, you've got a few choices that range from letting pop-ups be seen from certain websites to choosing how strict you want Internet Explorer 7 to be with pop-ups. Let's say that you've got a site you visit often (it could even be a company intranet site) and it uses pop-ups as a way to show more content without taking you away from the page you're looking at. That site is a good candidate to add to the Allowed Sites list so IE7 will no longer block pop-ups from that specific site. Just type in the address of the website at the top and click the Add button. The next section lets you pick whether you want IE7 to play a sound when pop-ups are blocked and whether you want to show an info bar at the top of the window when one is blocked. I suggest leaving these two settings on. Finally, you can choose a Filter Level from the pop-up menu. You've got three options: low, medium, or high. In a nutshell, the Low option means that IE7 will let more pop-ups be seen. The Medium option is the default, and it blocks most pop-ups. The High option will block all pop-ups—no matter where they come from or how important they may be. It's probably overkill for most. I find that the Medium option works best and does a good job of blocking pop-ups 90% of the time. When you're done changing any settings, click the Close button and IE7 will now use those options.

What Should You Do If You See This Dialog?

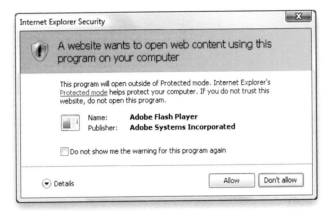

If you ever see this dialog, STOP! I know, I sound a little scary here but trust me, stop and think about it for a second before you click anything. This dialog pops up because the website you're visiting wants to install something on your computer. If you didn't click on anything to initiate the installation of software, then you'd probably better think about what this dialog says. Is it something that you want on your computer? This is one of the ways those nasty spyware companies trick people into installing their spyware. This dialog pops up when you just visit a site, and you unknowingly click Allow and the spyware gets installed. Now, that doesn't mean this dialog is all bad. In the example here, I visited a website that uses Flash technology to make the website more dynamic. That's usually a good thing and installing Adobe Flash Player, as in this example, is just fine. However, that's not always the case, so be careful when you see this dialog. Just stop and think for a moment to make sure that you do indeed want to install the program listed in the dialog.

What Is the Phishing Filter?

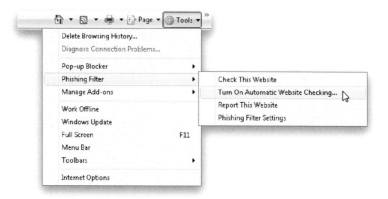

Phishing is covered in more detail in Chapter 6. It's in the email chapter because that's where phishing typically starts. However, I wanted to let you know of a feature in Internet Explorer 7 that helps protect against phishing should you not recognize it in an email. It's called the Phishing Filter, and it basically looks at the current website you're visiting and compares it against a list of known phishing website characteristics. If it detects that the website may be fraudulent, it'll pop up a warning dialog letting you know so you can close the page. Now, it's important to know the Phishing Filter is turned off by default, so if you want to turn it on, do this: in IE7, click on the Tools button and choose Phishing Filter from the pop-up menu. When the submenu pops up, you'll see a few options, but there's really only two that you'll want to know about: First, if you don't want to keep the Phishing Filter on all the time, you can keep it turned off by default and only check an individual page by choosing Check This Website. Now, if you want to keep it on all the time (which is what I do), then choose Turn On Automatic Website Checking. This will keep the Phishing Filter constantly on so it checks every site you visit.

RSS Feeds and IE7
(What Is an RSS Feed?)

If you already know what an RSS feed is, then just skip this tip and go to the next page to find out how Internet Explorer 7 helps you manage them. If not, then let me try to give you a quick explanation. An RSS (Really Simple Syndication) feed is a specially formatted document that summarizes the content of a website. Have you ever been to one of the popular news websites—CNN, Fox News, or even ESPN? Or your favorite blog websites? Well these sites broadcast their content in RSS. When you visit the website, you'll see the latest headlines formatted nicely with text and graphics all around. However, the driving content behind all of that is the feed. When it's formatted in the RSS format, that means that it's broadcast out to everyone to download independent from the website. For you, this means you can view the content of the website without ever actually going to the website by subscribing to the RSS feed and using a reader that we'll talk about next.

How to Know If a Website Has an RSS Feed

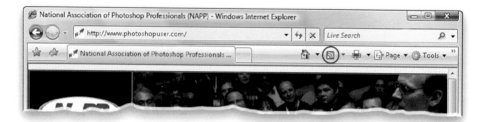

To see whether a website has an RSS feed, first visit the website. Let's use the two websites above as examples. Internet Explorer 7 will automatically search the site for RSS feeds. You'll be able to tell if the site has one by looking in the top toolbar. Look at the button to the right of the little Home button. This is the Feeds button. If it's gray when you visit the website, then that site does not offer an RSS feed. If it's orange, though, as you can see above in the capture of the Fox News website, then it does and you can subscribe to that feed.

Subscribing to an RSS Feed with IE7

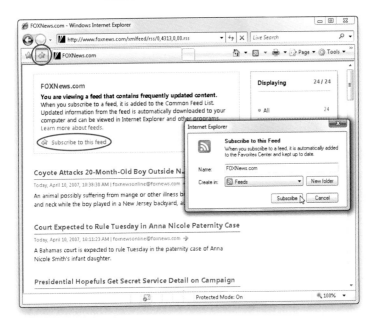

Once you confirm (by seeing an orange Feeds button) that the site does offer an RSS feed, click on the button. This will take you to the RSS feed page. Then click the Subscribe to This Feed button on the left side of the toolbar (it's a star with a green plus sign, and also serves as the Add to Favorites button) and choose Subscribe to This Feed, or click on the Subscribe to This Feed link at the top of the webpage. Either way, you'll get a dialog asking you to name the feed and choose what folder you want to place it in. When you're done, press the Subscribe button to subscribe to the feed. Now Internet Explorer 7 will automatically check the website's RSS feed and update it continually, so you never actually have to visit the website again to see what's going on.

TIP

To change how often an RSS feed updates, click on the Tools button in IE7's toolbar, and choose Internet Options. On the Content tab, under Feeds, click on the Settings button to get the Feed Settings dialog. Then, change the frequency on the Every pop-up menu.

Viewing Your RSS Feeds

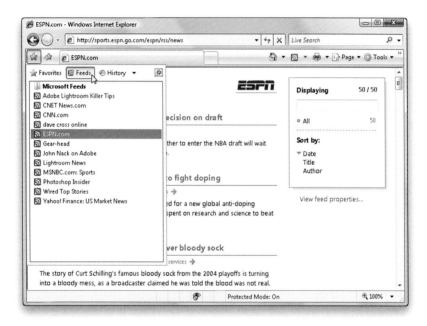

There are two ways to view RSS feeds. The first is through your Internet Explorer 7 Favorites list and the second is through a gadget (my favorite way). Let's look at the IE7 way first. Click on the Favorites button on the left side of the toolbar (the yellow star button). Then right below the button, you'll see three more buttons—Favorites, Feeds, and History. Click Feeds and the panel below will show the RSS feeds that you've subscribed to. To view one in your browser, just click on the feed. On the next page, we'll take a look at my favorite way to view RSS feeds.

Viewing RSS Feeds in a Gadget

This is my favorite way to view RSS feeds. First, be sure your Sidebar is open on your desktop and Right-click in an empty area on it. Choose Add Gadgets, and a new window with all available gadgets will open (for more on gadgets, make sure you check out Chapter 3). One of the default gadgets is Feed Headlines. Go ahead and Right-click on it and choose Add. This places the gadget into the Sidebar. Now you'll need to tell the gadget what feed you want it to display, so Right-click on the gadget itself and choose Options. A small Feed Headlines dialog will open, and all you need to do is change the Display This Feed pop-up menu to whichever feed you want to see. Click OK, and that gadget will now always show the headlines of the feed you set it to.

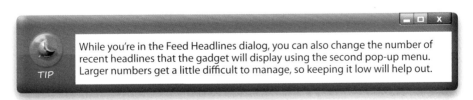

TIP

While you're in the Feed Headlines dialog, you can also change the number of recent headlines that the gadget will display using the second pop-up menu. Larger numbers get a little difficult to manage, so keeping it low will help out.

Viewing Browser History

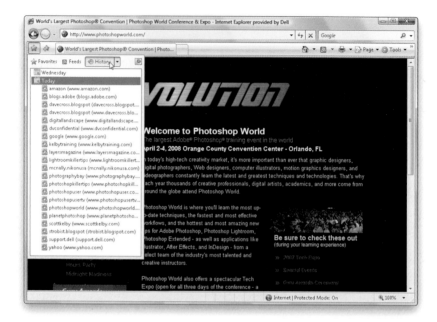

Internet Explorer 7's browser History file holds the websites that your Web browser has been to. It records each site visited and holds that information in its History file for 20 days by default. Many times I won't bookmark a website I'm on. Then a few weeks later, I wish I had because I can't find it anymore. That's where the History feature comes in handy because you can go back and look for it. To see the browser history, click the **Favorites** button on the far-left side of the toolbar. This displays three more buttons right below it. The one on the right is History. Click on it and you'll see your website history appear in the panel below. It'll be categorized into headings like Today, Monday, Last Week, or even 3 Weeks Ago. Just click on one of those headings to expand it and view the sites that fall within that time period.

TIP

Viewing your browser history is a great way to find a site that you forgot to book-mark. However, it's also a nice parental control. Say you haven't created your child their own Internet account or they happen to hop on the computer using your account. You can always double-check to see what they've been up to by looking at the browser history.

Clearing Your Browser History

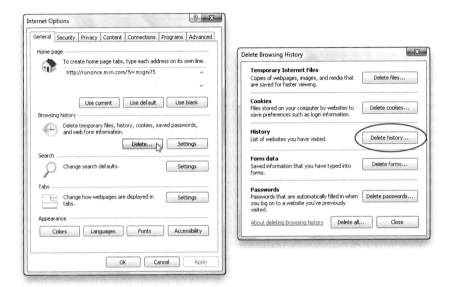

As you may already know, Internet Explorer stores a history of all of the websites that you visit. Sometimes this is a good thing because you may forget an important website, but if it's in IE7's history, you can always get back to it. That said, sometimes you may want to clear the history for privacy purposes. In IE7, click on the Tools button and choose Internet Options from the pop-up menu. On the General tab in the Internet Options dialog, under Browsing History, click the Delete button. Another dialog called Delete Browsing History will open. Under the History section, click the Delete History button and IE7 will remove its saved history of all the websites you've visited up to that moment. Keep in mind that it will start keeping track of your history once again from that point, so you'll have to go in there periodically to remove the history if that's something you need to do.

Internet Explorer 7 and Add-Ons

Add-ons are little programs that enhance the features of Internet Explorer 7. They can help you get things done faster, easier, or funner (is that really a word?). Really though, add-ons are just a browser-improving experience and they're great for personalizing the way you use IE7. Some are free, while you have to pay for others. To use an add-on is simple. First you need to download one, and the best place to start is the ones trusted by Microsoft itself. Go to www.windowsmarketplace.com and click on the IE Add-Ons button near the top-right corner of the homepage. Let's walk through downloading one of my favorites—it's called RoboForm2Go. This add-on is great for automatically filling out long web forms online, because it'll save your information for you and fill it in automatically, and it's portable with a USB flash drive. If it doesn't show up on the add-on homepage, you can just type RoboForm into the Search field at the top. Once you find it (or whatever other add-on you're downloading), click on the Free Download button (or Download Free Trial button) on the right side of the page. You'll have to sign in to Windows Marketplace even though this is free. If you don't have an account, then go ahead and create a free one by clicking the Sign Up Now button. Once you're signed in, you can download the add-on into your Downloads folder. Then, double-click on it to install it into IE7 and you're done.

Page Zoom

Statistics show that one out of every four people in the U.S. has an eyesight problem that makes it difficult to see text and graphics on websites. Being in that 25% myself makes this tip hit home. When I'm not wearing contact lenses, my glasses are so thick that I'm not allowed near trees and wooded areas on sunny days. I'm constantly squinting at the text on webpages. Well, Internet Explorer 7 has a new zoom feature that lets you zoom in on the text and graphics on a webpage. Even better, it uses a new magnification method that makes the graphics look better than ever when they're blown up. To use page zoom, go to the bottom-right corner of your IE7 window. There you'll see a little magnifying glass with 100% next to it. If you click on this Change Zoom Level button, you'll jump to 125%; click again and you'll jump to 150%. Or, click the little down-facing arrow next to it and you'll see various magnification levels to choose from. Just click on one and everything in your browser will be resized. So, if you have trouble seeing small text or graphics on your favorite websites, then get used to this one—it'll save your eyesight, and plenty of headaches.

TIP

Once you get the hang of using the page zoom feature, you can forgo clicking in the zoom area at the bottom right and just press the keyboard shortcut Ctrl–+ (plus sign) or Ctrl–– (minus sign) to zoom in and out respectively.

Turning Parental Controls On

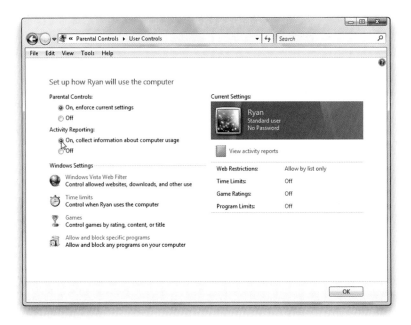

If you're a parent, you'll definitely want to read the next few pages. Vista includes built-in parental controls that help you keep tabs on the content, programs, and amount of time your children spend on the computer. Even if your child is an angel, it's the other people on the Internet that you have to watch out for. Websites often disguise themselves as something else and can be very misleading. Plus, children like some degree of autonomy and don't want you standing right next to them the whole time. To help guard against content your child shouldn't be viewing but, at the same time, give them the privacy they want, Vista has some very nice parental controls. These features include reports that help you watch over what your child is doing on the Web even if you can't be right next to them. To turn the parental controls on, go to Start>Control Panel>User Accounts and Family Safety. Click on Parental Controls. The next window asks you to choose a user to set the parental controls for. You'll need to have your children set up as separate user accounts on your machine. If you all use the same account, it doesn't really work because you'll just be blocking your own account and it'll cause you plenty of grief. Once you create another account, you'll see it in this window. Click on the account (in my case, I'll use my son Ryan) that you want to turn the parental controls on for. Under Parental Controls, turn on the option to enforce current settings. If you want reports (and trust me, I think you do), turn on the next option to enable activity reporting. That's it—parental controls are now on. Read the next few tips to find out how to use them to monitor your child's surfing time and habits.

Restricting Websites Automatically

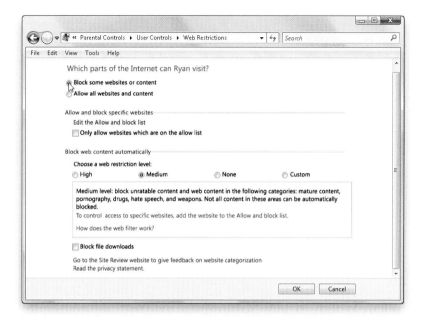

Website restrictions work in two ways: First, you, as the administrator of the computer, decide whether you want to add sites that the child is allowed to view or let Vista filter them automatically by content. Then, as he surfs the Web, your child will undoubtedly come upon websites that are okay to surf but are not on the "allowed" list. That's where you step in and give the okay. Here's how it works: Go to the same User Controls screen that was in the previous tip (Start>Control Panel>User Accounts and Family Safety> Parental Controls>Username). In this case, we'll use my son Ryan's account. In the Windows Settings section, click on Windows Vista Web Filter. At the top of the window, Vista asks you which parts of the Internet Ryan can visit. You'll choose Block Some Web-sites or Content. Under that, you'll see a section for Allow and Block Specific Websites. Here's where you need to make a decision. Do you want to have total control over the sites this user visits or do you want to let Vista manage it automatically using a Web filter? The Web filter gives websites a rating and blocks much of the objectionable content you'd normally want to keep from your child. However, it's not foolproof. I can't tell you which to choose because it really depends on the age and trustworthiness of your child, so you need to decide if it works for you. If it does, then leave the Only Allow Websites Which Are on the Allow List checkbox turned off, and choose a restriction level from the options under Block Web Content Automatically. If this method doesn't work for you, then check out the next tip to choose the sites your child can view.

Blocking and Allowing Specific Websites

If you really need to lock down the sites your child can view, then this tip is the one you want. First get to the Web Restrictions window (Start>Control Panel>User Accounts and Family Safety>Parental Controls>Username). Then, under Allow And Block Specific Websites, turn on the checkbox for Only Allow Websites Which Are on the Allow List. Now, at this point there isn't anything on the allow list so you'll need to start adding websites. To do this, click the Edit the Allow and Block List link to open the Allow or Block Specific Websites window. The rest is easy. In the Website Address field, just type the Web address you want to allow or block and click the appropriate button. You'll see it appear in the list below.

TIP

Children (especially teens) have a knack for downloading every piece-of-junk download you can imagine out there. These downloads can not only be viruses or spyware that'll wreak havoc on their computer, but guess who's going to get called to come fix it? So, you may want to consider turning on the Block File Downloads option in the Web Restrictions page.

Restricting the Time

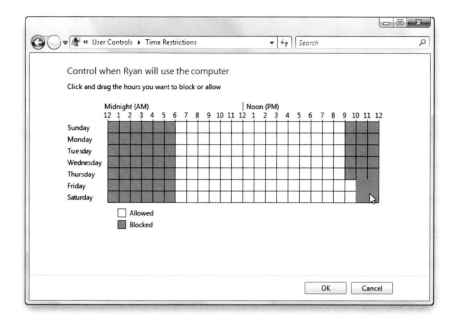

While you can't control the exact amount of time your kids spend online surfing, you can control the amount of time that they spend on the computer, which can work just as well. Go to the User Controls window (Start>Control Panel>User Accounts and Family Safety>Parental Controls>Username). Under Window Settings, click on the Time Limits link. This opens the Time Restrictions window. By default everything is white, which means there are no restrictions. If you want to restrict times that your child can use the computer, just click on a box (or click-and-drag on multiple boxes) in the grid. This is especially useful if you don't want them using the computer or Web after school or in the middle of the night when no one is nearby to oversee them. Click OK, and your time limits will be imposed. Your child will not be able to log into their account during those times. If they are on the computer when the time approaches, then they will automatically be logged off. Cruel, I know, but effective if you've got a computer junkie in the making.

Restricting Programs

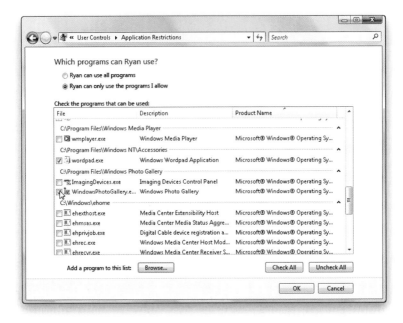

If you find you really need to lock your child down from the Web, but don't want to re-strict his time on the computer to do school work, then restricting the programs he can use may be effective. For example, you can restrict an account from using Windows Media Player or a popular instant messaging program but allow Microsoft Word or Windows Photo Gallery. So he can still write his paper, but can't listen to music, watch videos, or chat with friends. To enable this option, go to the User Controls window (Start>Control Panel>User Accounts and Family Safety>Parental Controls>Username). Under Window Settings, click on the Allow and Block Specific Programs link at the bottom to open the Applications Restrictions window. Click on Username Can Only Use the Programs I Allow (again, I'm using my son Ryan's account here). When you click that option, a list will pop up below. Now all that's left to do is turn on the check-boxes for the programs you want to enable this user to use. If you don't see the program you want in the list, then click on the Browse button at the bottom to browse for it. When you're done, click OK to close the window and those programs will now be the only programs your child can use.

Viewing Reports

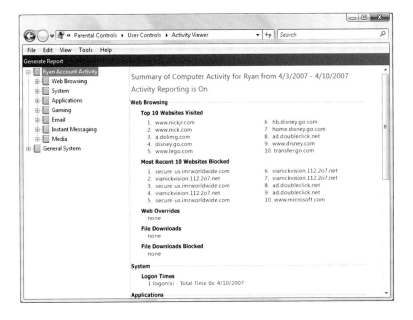

The last thing we'll cover here is viewing reports. Remember earlier in this chapter when I suggested you turn Activity Reporting on? Well, if you turned it on (I'm sure you listened to me), you can view these reports to see what your angelic offspring have been up to. To view the reports, go to the User Controls window (Start>Control Panel>User Accounts and Family Safety>Parental Controls>Username). Then click on the View Activity Reports link right under the account name in the top right of the window. The next window is the Activity Viewer, and I've got to tell you—this is one cool feature. You can see everything that the user has been up to. And when I say everything, I mean everything. Right down to log on/off times, email, instant messaging, and the music that they've listened to. You'll see the report stats on the right side of the screen but if you really want to zone in on a specific area just click the tree view on the left side. You can see the information for the user you're looking at as well as general system information. It's very cool and very detailed.

CHAPTER SIX

Keeping in Touch
Email and Instant Messaging

The first thing that's really going to make you feel at home in Vista is getting your email set up. It's like moving into a new house and unpacking all of your clothes—it just makes you feel better when it's done. Once your email is set up, then you start to feel like things are getting back to normal and you can now communicate with people again. So, we've devoted a whole chapter to getting your email set up, as well as showing you what's new/good/cool in Vista's new mail program, Windows Mail. (Pssst. By the way, Windows Mail is the replacement for Outlook Express, so don't freak out if you don't see your old email friend there.)

Windows Mail—
Where'd Outlook Express Go?

This may only sound like the title of a tip here, but it's actually the name of the new email program that comes with Windows Vista. Yep, it's time to say so long to Outlook Express and hello to Windows Mail. Have no worries though, Windows Mail does everything that Outlook Express did and more. It includes everything you need to send, receive, and manage your email. Plus, it has enhanced search capabilities for searching for that one email you just can't seem to find. It also includes better junk mail (or spam) filtering, a phishing filter (see the tip later in this chapter for more on what phishing is and why it's bad), and overall a better interface for managing your mail. Plus, for all of you Outlook Express users out there, you can import your contacts and email from Outlook Express (we'll talk about that later in this chapter) so you can be up and running right away. You get to Windows Mail by going to the Start menu. If you look up at the top-left side of the menu you'll see two icons—Internet and E-mail. Click on E-mail and that'll launch the new Windows Mail program.

TIP

If you're a Microsoft Outlook user (notice I didn't include the Express?), then you're not left out. While you can always use Windows Mail if you'd like, there is also a new version of Outlook called Outlook 2007. It comes with Microsoft Office 2007 (just like Outlook used to come with earlier versions of Microsoft Office). So, if you've got to use Outlook, then you'll need to install Office as well.

Importing Your Contacts

If you've already upgraded to Vista and you used to use Outlook Express, then you'll probably want to import your contacts from your old account. Keep in mind, this is when you've already upgraded, not while you're in the process of upgrading. First, you'll need to make sure you have a few things: (1) you'll need access to your old computer that has the mail, and (2) you'll need some type of storage (CD or DVD) to store the information on. Okay, now that you're ready, the first step is to go to Outlook Express on your old computer and choose File>Export. Export your Address Book here to a Text File (Comma Separated Values) file, then save that information by burning it to a CD or DVD, or even an external USB drive or hard drive. Next, go into Vista and open Windows Mail by going to the Start menu and choosing E-mail (Windows Mail) in the top left. Once Windows Mail launches, go to the File menu and choose Import>Windows Contacts. You'll see a new dialog pop open asking you what file format your contacts are in. If they're from Outlook Express, then choose the CSV (Comma Separated Values) format and click Import. The next window that opens lets you look for the location of your contacts file. This is the location you exported them to from Outlook Express. So, if it's on a CD or DVD, then insert the disc and navigate to it, or if it's on an external drive of some sort, then attach the drive and point to it there. When you've found the file location, click Next, and choose the fields you wish to import. Click Finish, and your contacts will start importing into Windows Mail.

Importing Old Email Messages

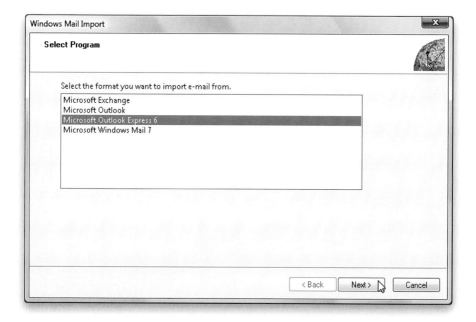

If you're like most people, you probably keep old email messages around for a while. Every once in a while you'll file them and their contents in places they belong but let's face it, our Inboxes tend to be the filing cabinet for many things in our lives. So it makes sense that if you start using Windows Mail, you'll want your email Inbox to follow. It actually works a lot like transferring your contacts does. Just open Windows Mail and go to the File menu. Choose Import>Messages. A dialog will open asking you which format you want to import messages from. Chances are it'll be Microsoft Outlook Express 6 or maybe even Microsoft Outlook. Choose your format based on which email program you used to use and click Next. The next window prompts you for a location of your exported messages (just like contacts, you'll need to export your messages first from your old email program). Find the file and click OK. Windows Mail will start the import process. When it's done, your Inbox will now have the same messages in it that were in your old email program, and life will be back to normal.

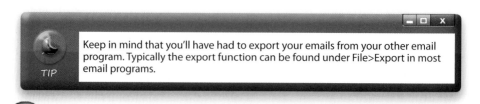

Keep in mind that you'll have had to export your emails from your other email program. Typically the export function can be found under File>Export in most email programs.

TIP

Setting Up an Email Account

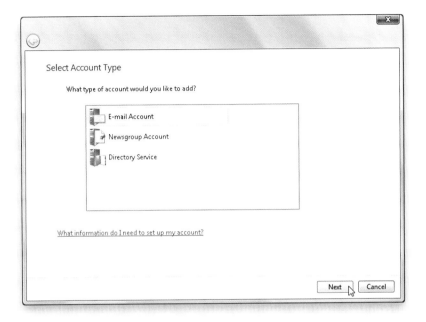

If you've got a new computer with Vista or want to set up a second email account, then in Windows Mail, go to the Tools menu and click Accounts. When the Internet Accounts dialog opens, click the Add button on the top right. You'll see a dialog asking what type of account you'd like to create. Choose E-mail Account and click the Next button. The first piece of information you'll be asked for is the name to display on the account. This isn't an official name for your account settings and security—it's just the name people will see when they receive an email from you. It can be a full name, first name only, or even a business name. Click Next and type the email address for this account. Click Next again to get to the really important settings: the ones that tell Windows Mail how to communicate with your email server or Internet Service Provider. When you signed up with your ISP, you should have gotten the server names, a user ID, and a password. This is the place to enter those server names (usually something like "something.server.com"), and click Next. Then, enter your username and password and click Next. In the final dialog, just click Finish to add the account. Now, Windows Mail will use the account you just added.

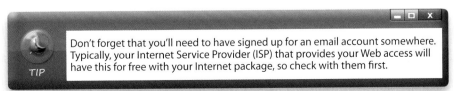

TIP

Don't forget that you'll need to have signed up for an email account somewhere. Typically, your Internet Service Provider (ISP) that provides your Web access will have this for free with your Internet package, so check with them first.

Creating Signatures

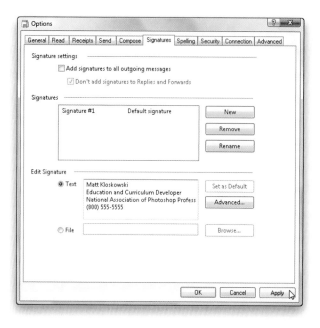

What do you do when you finish writing a letter (like anyone writes letters anymore, right?)? You sign it. Well, the same holds true for email, except instead of signing with a pen you sign with your keyboard by typing some closing remark and your name (maybe even your phone number, website, company name, etc.). Windows Mail, like most email programs, has a signature setting that will automatically sign your emails for you. You can turn it on so it always signs your emails no matter what, or you can selectively sign them when you want. You can even create multiple signatures—one for friends and one for business contacts. But before you start using signatures, you need to create one. In Windows Mail, go to the Tools menu and choose Options. When the Options dialog opens, click on the Signatures tab. If you've never created a signature before, then the Signatures field in this tab will be empty. To add a signature, click the New button on the right side. This puts a new signature entry in the Signatures field. You'll see your cursor blinking in the Edit Signature Text field below. That's where you type your closing remarks and your name, company name, title, phone number, etc. When you're done, click Apply to commit the changes. Now you can add another signature if you'd like (maybe one for home and one for work purposes) or just click OK.

Adding a Signature to an Email

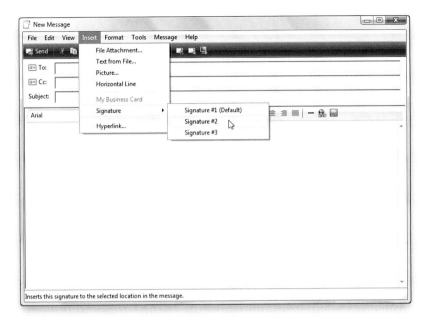

Once you've created your signature(s), you have a few options for how to use it. First you can choose to automatically add it to your new emails by turning on the Add Signatures to All Outgoing Messages checkbox at the top of the Signatures tab when you're creating the signature. You can, however, leave that option off and add it manually when you create the email. I actually like this option best because I have several signatures I use depending on whom I'm sending email to. If it's someone I'm just making contact with, I have a signature that has all of my information. I don't include it in every email though, only the first time. I have another signature for emails to friends, and one for emails to business acquaintances too. To manually add your signature, go ahead and click the Create Mail button to create a new email. Then, in the New Message dialog, go to the Insert menu and choose Signature. Pick the signature from the list if you've got more than one, and it'll be added to the email. This way you get to choose whether or not to include the signature in the email.

Emailing Photos to Your Family and Friends

Have you ever sent or received a photo in an email from someone and the photo took up the entire screen? You most likely couldn't even see the whole photo without scrolling. It's a very common problem, especially with the size of photos coming out of digital cameras these days. Now, you probably already know you can attach photos to an email. Just click the little paper clip icon in the toolbar of your message window. However, Vista has another cool way to attach photos to an email and it gives you the control to choose what size to attach the photo at. Oddly enough, it's not in the message window. Instead, go to the Start menu and choose Pictures on the right side. Locate the folder that has the photos you want to send. If you didn't put your photos in the Pictures folder, then go ahead and locate them in Windows Explorer (also, you may want to read the tip in Chapter 7 about Autoplay and why you should start putting photos in the Pictures folder). Okay, now click on the photo that you want to send. In the toolbar, you'll see an E-mail button. Click on that and the Attach Files dialog opens. The only setting here is Picture Size. Choose the size you want from the pop-up menu and click Attach. Vista will create a new email with the photo attached to it and all you'll need to do is choose the person you want to send it to and include a message.

Changing the Amount of Time
Windows Mail Waits to Check for Email

By default, Windows Mail in Vista waits 30 minutes to check for new email messages. Personally, I think that's a bit too long, hence this tip. Now, you can always click the Send/Receive button in the toolbar if you want to check manually, but the whole idea is to let your computer do the work for you. So, if you'd like to change the amount of time that Windows Mail waits to check for email, just go to the Tools menu and choose Options. When the Options dialog opens, it'll automatically be set to the General tab. Under Send/Receive Messages, you'll see an option for Check for New Messages Every, with the default setting of 30 minutes. You can adjust the 30 minutes setting to whatever you'd like. I set mine to 5 minutes, and that way Windows Mail is constantly checking for new email messages. Click OK when you're done to close the dialog and the new setting will take effect.

Managing Junk Mail

Unfortunately for all of us, junk mail (a.k.a. spam) is a fact of life these days and it's not going away, at least not without some help. Windows Mail includes a new junk mail filter to help alleviate the problem. It's turned on by default, but you can get to it to adjust the settings by going to the Tools menu and choosing Junk E-mail Options. Here you have a few options. First, you can turn off junk mail protection altogether. Next, you can set it to Low, which will block the obvious junk mail but will definitely let some through to your Inbox as well. This is the default setting and typically what I keep mine set to. Then there is the High setting, which will block most of the junk mail but you'll likely get some of your regular email blocked as well. Next, there is the Safe List Only setting. This one only lets email from people that you've got on your Safe Senders List (see the next two tips for more on this) through to your Inbox. That means, if you don't tell Windows Mail that a certain sender is okay, then everything they send (and I mean *everything*) will be blocked. Finally, at the bottom of the dialog is an option to permanently delete suspected junk mail instead of moving it to the Junk E-mail folder. I personally leave this option off because I prefer to periodically check my junk folder for important emails that may have inadvertently gotten sent there. After you've chosen a setting, click OK to close the dialog and accept the changes.

What to Do If Junk Mail Still Gets Through to Your Inbox

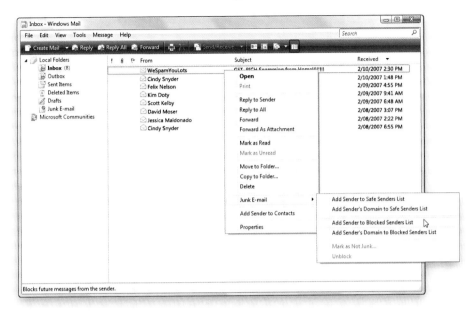

If you find an email that really should have been sent to your Junk E-mail folder, you can easily send it there and tell Windows Mail not to let that person through to the Inbox again. When you see the junk email in your Inbox, Right-click on it and choose Junk E-mail>Add Sender to Blocked Senders List. This will put the sender into a list of blocked email addresses whose emails will always get sent to the Junk E-mail folder. You'll see another option called Add Sender's Domain to Blocked Senders List. This option is a little different. For example, let's say you get a junk email from janeisapain@yahoo.com. If you simply add the sender to the Blocked Senders List, then emails from janeisapain@yahoo.com will always go to the Junk E-mail folder. However, if you add the sender's domain to the Blocked Senders List, then emails from anyone @yahoo.com will be sent there, even if it's someone who happens to be your friend. So, be careful with that option. If you see an email like john@ilovetosendspam.com, then go ahead and block the whole domain, but beware of blocking domains you recognize or some of your friends may get blocked too.

TIP

If you accidentally block a sender that you didn't want to, just choose Tools>Junk E-mail Options. Go to the Blocked Senders tab and click on the name you think should be safe. Then, click the Remove button to take them off the Blocked Senders List.

What to Do If a Good Email Actually Gets Sent to the Junk E-mail Folder

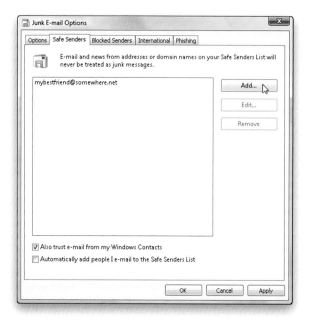

There are two ways to keep people you know from getting sent to the Junk E-mail folder. First, every once in a while an email will get flagged as junk that really isn't. That's why it's good to look in the Junk E-mail folder to make sure that a real email didn't accidentally get sent there. If you do find an email that was flagged as junk but shouldn't be, then you'll want to tell Windows Mail that the sender is safe. To do that, Right-click on the email itself and choose Junk E-mail>Mark as Not Junk. A dialog will open asking if you want to add this sender to the Safe Senders List. I typically choose yes so they don't get flagged as junk later on. The next way to keep email from people you know from getting sent to the Junk E-mail folder is to add them to your Safe Senders List. Go to the Tools menu and choose Junk E-mail Options. In that dialog, click on the Safe Senders tab. Click on the Add button, type the email address of the person you'd like to add to the list in the Add Address or Domain dialog, and click OK. You can edit or remove an existing address using the two buttons below the Add button. Click OK, and emails from the addresses you added will always go to your Inbox regardless of their message content.

TIP

At the bottom of the Safe Senders tab is an option to always trust email from your Windows Contacts. These are people that you've put into your contact list, and I'd suggest turning this option on if it's not already. After all, if you've taken the time to add them as a contact, then you don't want to miss any email from them.

Mail Rules or Filters

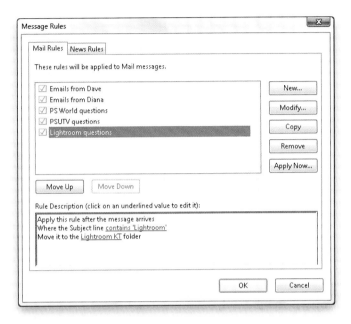

If you're having trouble managing large amounts of email, then rules (or Message Rules, as Vista calls them) are the answer. A Message Rule is something you set up to automatically process incoming emails. You can have your incoming emails sent to a specific folder (or set to a variety of other actions like forwarding it or deleting it) based on the email message's sender, subject, message body, CC names, priorities, etc. A good example of a rule is that whenever my boss sends me an email, I want it to go to a folder that I've set up to hold my boss's email messages. That way, when I need to get to messages from him I can go straight to one place. I've got rules set up for everything from the people I work with, to my wife and family, as well as newsletters and alerts that I subscribe to. That way, my Inbox stays clutter-free and I always know where to go first when I'm reading mail. If you haven't used Message Rules, then you really owe it to yourself to try them. If you're receiving a lot of email each day, then they help you manage the email, as well as prioritize which ones you're going to deal with right away, while keeping the ones that may not be quite as important from stealing your attention.

Setting Up Rules

Setting up a mail rule is a breeze. First you'll need to create a folder to hold the emails. Right-click on your Local Folders at the top of the list on the left side of your Windows Mail window and choose New Folder. For my example, I'll add a folder named "Dave" (my boss's name) and click OK. Obviously, your boss probably isn't named Dave, so you'll pick another name. Now go to Tools>Message Rules>Mail. In step 1, choose the condition for the rule. In this case, the condition will be the top one: Where the From Line Contains People. In step 2, choose the action you want to take place when the email arrives. Here I want the email to be moved to a specific folder, so choose that action. Now, in step 3, you need to specify the people and folders you want this rule to apply to. Click on the highlighted and underlined text that reads "contains people" and type the name of the person you want to apply the rule to or click Contacts and choose the person there. Click OK when you're done to return to the New Mail Rule dialog. Then click the word "specified" to choose a folder to send these messages to. Click on the name of the folder in the Move dialog and click OK. Finally, at the bottom, give your rule a descriptive name like "Emails from Dave" so it's easy to find later. Click OK to accept all of your changes and now whenever you get an email from the person you specified, it'll be moved to the folder that you created for that person.

What Is Windows Calendar?

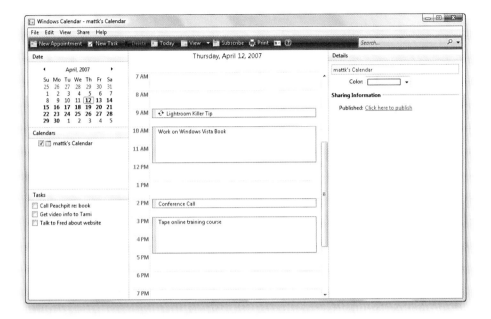

Windows Calendar is a very cool little application that comes with Windows Vista to help manage your life. I've got to admit that this is a pretty sweet little program for being free operating system software. It does everything from managing your appointments and alerting you to when they're coming up, to keeping track of your tasks, as well as keeping tabs on important dates such as birthdays and anniversaries. You can launch Windows Calendar by going to the Start menu, to All Programs. Then, click on Windows Calendar to launch it. It's very straightforward to use, so give it a try. Like I said before, it's a sweet program considering it's free with Vista.

Changing Your Calendar View

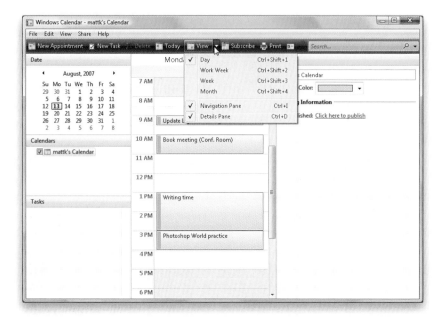

By default, when you open Windows Calendar, your calendar shows you the current day's view from morning until evening. If you've got a lot of appointments and meetings during the day, this may be the best view for your calendar. However, you can change it by clicking the View button. If you click on the down-facing arrow to the right of the View button, you'll see a pop-up menu with an option for Work Week, which shows you just Monday through Friday and has smaller time slots for each hour of the day. Then there's Week, which is the same, except it shows Saturday and Sunday, too. Finally, there's the Month option, which shows you the entire month. You don't get to see all of the time slots that you would in one of the other options, but if you're more concerned with glancing at the "main event" for each day rather than managing meetings and appointments, it may be the best one for you.

Keeping Track of Your To Dos

Windows Calendar also has a task list that'll function as your to-do list. It's not quite the same, but it's pretty darn close and comes in really handy. If you're used to using a piece of paper for your to dos, then the task list can be a lifesaver. For starters, it never gets lost. You can also set up a reminder to alert you when one of the to dos needs to get done, so you don't forget. To start off, make sure that you can see your Navigation Pane by choosing View>Navigation Pane (or just press Ctrl-I). It's the area on the left side of the screen that shows the month view of your calendar, as well as the Tasks pane at the bottom left. When you start, you probably won't have any tasks (a.k.a. to dos), but if you click the New Task button at the top, you can create a brand new one. Give it a descriptive name like "Pick up dry cleaning." Then look over to the right side of the screen at the Details pane. Here, you can enter any details that have to do with that task such as due date, notes, or even a reminder, which pops open a little reminder window when your task is due. Finally, when you complete one of your tasks, just click on the checkbox next to it in the Tasks pane so you know it's now off your to-do list.

What Are Calendar Subscriptions?

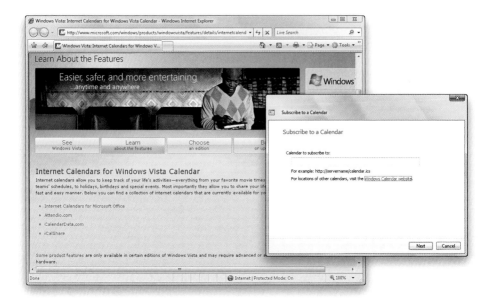

If you take one thing from this calendar section, I hope it's this tip on subscriptions. With Windows Calendar, you can subscribe to free calendars on the Web. For example, if you're a football fan there are free calendars available that automatically place the dates and times of football games into your calendar. I'm a big fan of the TV shows *Entourage* and *Lost* (although I usually have more questions at the end of each show than at the beginning). You can subscribe to calendars that add your favorite shows to your calendar so you don't miss new episodes. There are hundreds of calendars for everything you can think of—from your favorite bands' tour dates to Holistic Health in Central Ohio. I'm tellin' you, these things are awesome, and save the time you'd take inputting all of those dates manually. If you're new to these types of calendars, it's easy to get started. They're typically in the iCal format (they have an ICS extension), and any calendar in that format works with Windows Calendar. Just click on the Subscribe button in the Windows Calendar toolbar, and either enter the Web address of a calendar or click on the Windows Calendar Website link to find some. Many sites automatically download the calendar for you.

TIP

If you're new to public calendars, you've probably never heard of the iCal format. All you really need to know is that it's a public standard for creating calendars. A bunch of people got together and decided calendars should be in a certain format, and if everyone followed we could all share calendars, thus iCal was born.

Publishing Your Calendar

In much the same way that you subscribe to calendars created by other people, you too can create your own calendars and share them with co-workers or even on the Internet. You can even password protect your calendar so only certain people can view your schedule. If you want to publish your own calendar, the first step is to go in and update your calendar in Windows Calendar so it has something to see. Then go to the Share menu and choose Publish. Type the name of your calendar and then enter the location that you want to publish it to. If it's going onto a website, then enter the website directly. If you're going to manually send the calendar ICS file to someone, then just pick a location on your computer. If you want to automatically publish changes you make to the calendar without having to go through this process again, turn that checkbox on in the center of the dialog. Finally, at the bottom, turn on the checkboxes for any of the other settings pertaining to the types of details you want to publish with your calendar. When you're done, click Publish and Windows Calendar will create the ICS file for you and publish it to the location you chose.

Instant Messaging and Vista

Vista doesn't come with an instant messaging program when you install it. Back in XP, we used to have Windows Messenger that was installed by default. For Vista, the instant messaging program is called Windows Live Messenger and it's part of the Windows Live family. However, you'll have to download it first, so open a Web browser and go to http://get.live .com. On the left side of the page, you'll see Windows Live Messenger. Click that link to go to the Windows Live Messenger webpage and click the Try It button to start the download. Once it's done, go to your Downloads folder and double-click the Install_Messenger.exe icon to start the install of Windows Live Messenger.

What Phishing Is and Why It's Bad

Yep, you read the title correctly. The word is phishing with a "ph," but it's pronounced the same as the word fishing. You probably already know what phishing is even if you've never heard the term before. Phishing (another form of junk email) is when those unscrupulous folks who like to steal from people send out emails telling you that your bank account, credit card, PayPal account, or other type of account needs to be updated. These emails look very professional and like they're the "real thing," but they're not. They try to fool you into following a link to a website and entering your password and credit card number or bank account information so they can steal from you. It's bad stuff, but Windows Mail has a way to help. First, go to the Tools menu and choose Junk E-mail Options. Then click the last tab on the right, labeled Phishing. Make sure that the top checkbox is turned on so that any potential phishing emails will be flagged in your email Inbox. You can also tell Windows Mail to send them directly to your Junk Mail folder, so you don't even have to deal with them in your Inbox. One thing to keep in mind, though, is that this is ground zero when dealing with phishing, because it usually starts from an email. Internet Explorer 7 also has ways of dealing with it (covered in Chapter 5) should you end up at a website suspected of phishing.

CHAPTER SEVEN

Getting the Most Out of Your Photos

Viewing, Editing, and Printing

Pictures! We love them. I've got boxes of them in my home and I've got hard drives full of 'em on my desk. First, the boxes. I pretty much know what I'm supposed to do with those. Spread them out on the floor, put them into stacks or envelopes or groups to keep them organized, and put my favorite ones in an album. But what are we supposed to do with all of these digital photos? Windows Vista comes with a program called Photo Gallery that can be your one-stop shop for all your photo needs. First, it lets you import and organize them. Next, you can even apply some fixes to them (like brightening, darkening, or even creating black-and-white images), and finally, you can share them with other people in slide shows and emails. It's the program that Windows users who don't want to shell out the money or time to learn another program have been waiting for.

Getting Your Photos onto the Computer

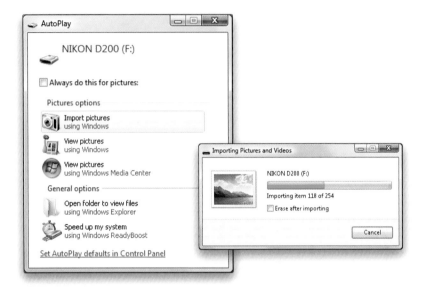

The easiest way to get your photos onto your computer is to connect your camera or memory card reader to your PC's USB port. When you do, the AutoPlay dialog automatically opens. Now, the AutoPlay dialog has gotten some bad press in the past. It's always popping up when you plug something in and that tends to annoy people (me, too). I used to be a control freak when it came to my computer and wanted to do things my own way. However, I've become more convinced that the way Windows prompts you to do things is actually easier. So I suggest using AutoPlay when possible. For example, getting photos onto your computer is the perfect time. When AutoPlay opens after you've connected your camera or card reader, the top option will be to Import Pictures. Go ahead and click on that. You'll be asked whether you want to apply tags to these photos automatically (see the tip later in this chapter for more info on using tags). If you want to apply a tag, then type it or choose it from the list. Either way, when you're ready, just click the Import button to start moving your photos onto your computer. You'll see a progress bar showing how many photos are left to import. You can also turn on the Erase After Importing checkbox to automatically erase the photos when it's done. Personally, I still retain some of my control-freakishness here and leave that option turned off. I like to make sure everything is all safe and sound before deleting my photos, so I do it manually when the import is done. Now, when the import is done, go to your Pictures folder to find the photos you've just imported. We'll talk about getting to them in Windows Photo Gallery next.

Turning AutoPlay On and Off

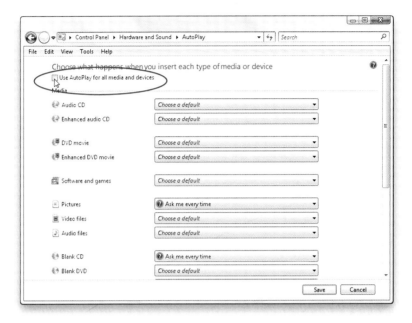

I'm including this tip because I know AutoPlay just annoys the living daylights out of some people. If you're one of them, then you can indeed turn off our beloved AutoPlay dialog so it doesn't pop up when you plug media-related devices into your computer. To do this, go to the Control Panel (Start>Control Panel) and click on Hardware and Sound. Then, click on the AutoPlay link. This will take you to a window that lets you adjust every aspect of how AutoPlay operates. However, if you want to turn it off altogether then turn off the Use AutoPlay for All Media and Devices checkbox. Now it's gone forever and it will never annoy you again (that is until someone turns that checkbox on again).

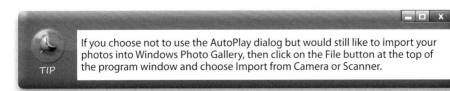

TIP

If you choose not to use the AutoPlay dialog but would still like to import your photos into Windows Photo Gallery, then click on the File button at the top of the program window and choose Import from Camera or Scanner.

Viewing Your Photos

MATT KLOSKOWSKI, ©ISTOCKPHOTO

In the old days of Windows XP, you were probably used to going to the folder that had your photos in Windows Explorer and viewing them there. It wasn't particularly easy, nor fun, to do it that way, but that's the way most people did it. Now, in Vista there's a better way. It's called Windows Photo Gallery and let me tell ya—this little program rocks! It's free with Vista and it's got some killer features for managing, organizing, viewing, and fixing your photos. If you imported your photos using the method described on the previous page (which I suggest you do), then you automatically imported them into the Pictures folder. Forget about the old days of going to Windows Explorer and trying to find the folder that had your photos. Now you'll go to Photo Gallery to see them. Go to the Start menu and choose Windows Photo Gallery. If you don't see it in the main list of programs, then just click on All Programs and it'll be in that list. When Photo Gallery opens, you'll see your photos in the center preview area.

Getting Your Photos into Windows Photo Gallery

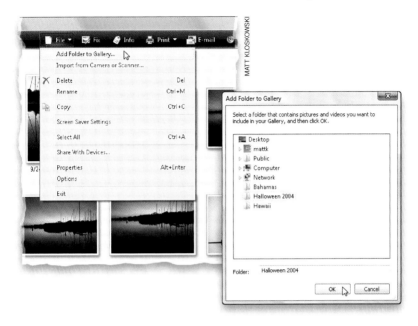

If you imported your photos into your Pictures folder, they're already there and just look at the previous tip for viewing them. However, one of two other things may have happened: (1) you decided to keep your photos where you want them and not where Vista suggests (in the Pictures folder), or (2) you bought this book after you already moved photos onto your computer and you put them into a different folder. In either case, let's just assume that you didn't put your photos into the Pictures folder and they're somewhere else on your computer. In that case, you won't see them in Windows Photo Gallery. But you want to, so you'll have to tell Photo Gallery where the pictures are. Go to the File menu, choose Add Folder to Gallery, then navigate to the folder they're in and choose it. This tells Vista that you want to view your photos in Photo Gallery so you have the ability to do all of the cool things we're about to talk about.

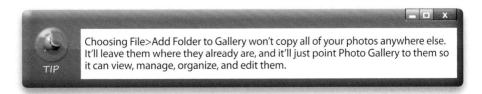

TIP

Choosing File>Add Folder to Gallery won't copy all of your photos anywhere else. It'll leave them where they already are, and it'll just point Photo Gallery to them so it can view, manage, organize, and edit them.

Increasing Thumbnail Size

Sometimes you may want to see more photos on the screen so you can quickly scroll through them to find the photo you need. Other times, you may want to see some larger thumbnails of the photos to see some of the details. Fortunately, you can pick which one of these views you want anytime, because Windows Photo Gallery has the ability to customize the thumbnail sizes you see. If you look along the bottom of the Photo Gallery window, you'll see a little magnifying glass with a plus sign on it on the left side of the tools. Click on that magnifying glass to open a pop-up slider. Dragging the slider upward will make your photo thumbnails larger. However, you won't be able to see as many onscreen. Dragging it downward will make them smaller. The tradeoff here is that, even though you can see more onscreen, you won't be able to see any of the details of the photos. So, if several photos are alike, they'll all tend to look the same when the thumbnails are smaller. Either way, it's good to know you have the option to make them the size you want.

TIP

To view RAW files in Windows Photo Gallery, go to your camera manufacturer's website and look for their RAW Codec file that works with your camera model and Windows Vista.

Editing and Fixing Photos

One of the reasons you're going to fall instantly in love with Windows Photo Gallery is the fact that you can actually fix some of the most common problems with your digital photos. Got photos that are too dark? There's a fix for it. Want a little color saturation boost? Got that, too. If your photos have red eye, need cropping, or just need some overall enhancement, then Photo Gallery is the first place you can turn. Don't get me wrong here, though. Adobe Photoshop it ain't. If you've got a head from Uncle John that you want to place onto your favorite pet, then Photo Gallery is definitely not the place to turn. It is, however, great for some common basic fixes for your photos as well as managing your photos altogether, and I think you're going to love it. To get started, just open Photo Gallery, click on a photo in the center preview area, and click the Fix button in the toolbar. When you get into the Fix pane, you'll see your photo very large onscreen and you'll see some settings over on the right. We'll talk about each one in more detail over the next few pages.

Fixing Photos That Are Too Dark or Too Light

MATT KLOSKOWSKI

Taking photos that are too dark or too light is probably one of the most common problems you'll run into. In photography terms, anything that deals with the lightness and darkness of the photo is generally called exposure, and there happens to be an Adjust Exposure fix in Windows Photo Gallery. Just click on a photo to select it in the center preview area, then click the Fix button in the top toolbar. Look over on the right side of the Fix pane and you'll see an Adjust Exposure button. Click on the button to expand it, and there will be two sliders: Brightness and Contrast. The Brightness slider does just what it says. If you move it to the right the photo will become brighter, and if you move it to the left it will become darker. So if your photo is too dark, then try moving this slider to the right to brighten it up. We'll cover contrast in the next tip, but after lightening a dark photo it's always good to bump that Contrast slider over to the right just a little to add a little more contrast.

Fixing Dull Photos

Dull photos are ones that lack overall contrast and just don't (as many call it) "pop." It happens with newer digital photos, but you'll really see it in older photos—especially the kind that you pull out of the shoebox and scan into your computer. Well, there's a great fix in Windows Photo Gallery to take care of these dull photos and it involves just one slider. So, once you find a dull photo try this: Click on the Fix button to go into Fix mode. Then click on Adjust Exposure. Underneath this, you'll now see the Contrast slider. Take that slider and move it toward the right to increase the contrast. Essentially you're taking the darkest parts of the photo and making them darker and the lightest parts of the photo and making them lighter (and leaving everything else in between alone). This improves the overall appearance of the photo and does a great job of making older, dull photos look much better.

Boosting Colors

©ISTOCKPHOTO/BEN BLANKENBURG

One of the biggest complaints I hear from people taking pictures is that the photo never looks like it did when they were there. Usually, the camera captures the moment pretty well, but the feeling we get from actually being there tends to enhance what we thought of the scene. A perfect example is the photo you see above. Before I enhanced it, the colors looked rather lifeless. It seemed to me that her hair and flowers should be more vibrant. All of the colors just seemed like they should be more saturated than they appeared on the computer. So, if you ever want to add a color boost to your photos, click on the Adjust Color button. Then, drag the Saturation slider to the right. Don't go crazy here by dragging it to the end. The nice saturation boost you get by dragging it about three-fourths of the way to the right will usually work great.

Making a Quick Black–and–White Photo

The Fix pane in Windows Photo Gallery has a nice easy way to create a quick black-and-white photo. If you haven't noticed, even though we have all of these options for enhancing beautiful color photos, there's something about those elegant black-and-white photos we always see. They give a photo an entirely different feel. If you'd like to create one in Photo Gallery, then click on a photo to select it and click on the Fix button to go into the Fix pane. Click on the Adjust Color setting on the right side to expand it. Take the Saturation slider and move it all the way to the left to totally remove any color from the photo. Now you have a black-and-white image. If you want to take this one a step further, go under the Adjust Exposure setting and start tweaking the Brightness and Contrast sliders, as well. You'll be amazed at how those two sliders can totally change the look and feel of your black-and-white photos.

Creating a Sepia-Tinted Photo

Another cool thing you can do with Windows Photo Gallery is tint your photos. In the Fix pane, click on Adjust Color, and in addition to the Saturation slider, you'll see a Color Temperature slider and a Tint slider. Moving the Color Temperature slider to the right adds a yellow tint to the photo (also called warming the photo). Moving it to the left adds a blue tint (also called cooling the photo). The Tint slider works much the same, except that moving it to the right adds a reddish color to the photo and moving it to the left adds a greenish tint. If you're looking for some ideas to try with these controls, then try this: First, move the Saturation slider all the way to the left to remove the color saturation from the photo. Now, you need to commit this change before doing anything else, so just click the Back To Gallery button to go back to the main window. Now, go and fix the same photo again. This time, under Adjust Color, start dragging the Color Temperature slider all the way to the right to make the photo yellow. How much is up to you. The more you drag it, the more yellow will be introduced and give you the appearance of an old sepia-tinted photo.

TIP

If you wanted to change the feeling of a photo—for example, making a photo that wasn't shot at sunrise appear as if it was—then try dragging the Color Temperature slider to the right and leaving everything else alone. That'll give it a nice, warm, morning sunrise feel.

Cropping Photos

©ISTOCKPHOTO/DUNCAN WALKER

The beautiful thing about shooting photos digitally is that we have so many more opportunities after the fact to make the photos look better. One of these is called cropping. Have you ever looked at a photo and thought that the people in the center of the photo were surrounded by too much space? After all, we want the photos of our friends and family to concentrate on them and show them as best we can. If there's too much space around them, you'll start to lose the feeling of a nice portrait and your photos will just look like snapshots. To help fix this, we can crop unwanted area from our photos by going into the Fix pane and clicking on Crop Picture. The first choice you'll need to make is under the Proportion setting. If you want free rein over the crop frame, then leave it as Custom and you can create any size or shape crop you like by clicking-and-dragging on any corner of the frame overlay. However, if you're going to be printing this photo, then you'll want to make sure you crop it based on the size print you'll be creating. For example, if you're printing a 5x7" photo, then change the Proportion setting to 5x7. This constrains your crop frame to this ratio, so no matter how much you drag each corner, it'll still look fine as a 5x7" photo. Alternatively, if you want to flip it and print a 7x5" photo instead, then just click the Rotate Frame button right below the Proportion pop-up menu. Okay, one more thing: aside from clicking-and-dragging the corners of the crop frame around, you can also click-and-drag the entire frame itself by putting your cursor inside of the frame and clicking-and-dragging there. Now you have total control over the final composition of your photos. Just click Apply when you're done to commit the settings.

Fixing Red Eye

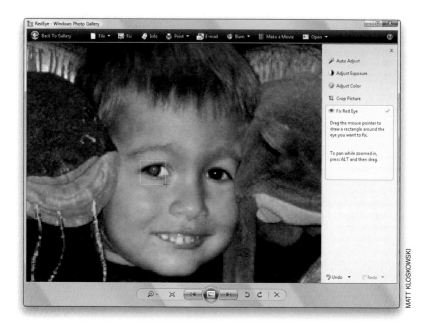

MATT KLOSKOWSKI

To wrap up our tips on the Windows Photo Gallery's Fix pane, we'll fix the dreaded red eye. Come on…you know it happens to your photos. In fact, I'll bet I can guess how. It's a rainy November night. The fog rolls in…okay, too spooky. Instead, picture this: It's late evening, or even nighttime, and you're having the family over for a birthday party. You pull out the camera and, with the flash off, you start snapping some pictures only to discover they're too dark. Or, better yet, your camera has auto flash, which senses that it's too dark, so it automatically turns the flash on. Now you take some pictures and things seem good enough. Then you load them onto your computer, only to find that everyone in the photos looks like a red-eyed demon. While I often think that of my kids from the way they act sometimes, you realize it's a red-eye problem because the unsuspecting adults look that way too. At this point, you probably read up on your camera to find that it has an auto red-eye block feature. What it does is flashes twice: once before the shot and once while it's taking the shot. Bad choice. What does everyone do after they see the flash? Walk away. They think they're done, so they start moving and now you've got lots of photos with people turned away. The answer is the Fix Red Eye feature in the Fix pane. Just select a red-eye photo and click the Fix button. In the Fix pane, click the Fix Red Eye button. Now, with your cursor, click-and-drag out a box around the red eye (you may need to zoom in on the eyes to see them better), and watch Photo Gallery automatically remove it just like that.

Rotating Photos

If one of your photos ever appears sideways when you're viewing it in Windows Photo Gallery, you can use the Rotate buttons to rotate it. You'll often find this if you flip your camera sideways to take a vertical shot instead of a landscape, or horizontal, one. If this happens, take a look in the bottom toolbar for the two little half circle arrow buttons. They're the Rotate Counterclockwise and Rotate Clockwise buttons. So, if your photo is rotated to where the top of the photo appears on the left side, then click the Rotate Clockwise button. If it's the opposite, then click the Rotate Counterclockwise button to get it straight. Each click will rotate the photo by 90°, or one turn, in the direction you click.

TIP

A quick, easy way to zoom in on your photos without having to go under any menus is to press Ctrl–+ (plus sign) or Ctrl–– (minus sign).

Organizing Photos in Windows Photo Gallery

First off, if you're not sure why you should bother organizing your photos, then think of this: Let's say I have a shoebox (or even a large box) full of photo prints saved over the years. I decide I want to find a photo of my son Justin from Christmas 2003. What do I do? Well, I look through the shoebox until I find the photo, right? If I only have 50 or 100 photos in there, then it's not so bad. But what if I have thousands? Then it's bad. Now, the organized type would have albums and would know right where to go to find those photos. That's kind of how it works on your computer. You can keep putting photos onto your hard drive and never organize them, but then when you go to find one, you'd better make sure you've got some time to devote to the searching process. Or you can use a few of the simple ways that Vista includes to help organize your photos. The good news for you is that Photo Gallery actually organizes your photos for you automatically (to a point). There also are some other ways that, with a little time spent by you, will totally change the way you view and find your photos forever. You'll be able to find photos you want immediately with just a few clicks. So, for the next few pages, that is what we're going to concentrate on: organizing and finding your photos quickly.

How Vista Organizes Your Photos Automatically

By just adding your photos to Windows Photo Gallery, you're already letting Vista organize your photos for you. When you open Photo Gallery, look at the Navigation pane on the left side to see the different ways your photos are organized. At the top, you have the option to view pictures and/or videos. Just click Pictures, so you don't see the videos anymore. They're not gone, you just won't see them in the center preview area. Below that, if you want to see photos that were imported last, click on Recently Imported. Next are Tags, which are hands-down the best way to organize your photos, but we'll cover those on the next few pages. Below that you have the second-best way to organize—Date Taken. You don't have to do a thing here. Photo Gallery does this for you as you import your photos. It starts by year, but you can click the right-facing arrow next to a year to see each month. You can also expand each month to see the days you shot photos. So, if you wanted to see photos from Christmas Eve 2006, you'd expand 2006, then expand December, and look for December 24th. Right below Date Taken is Ratings, where you can organize with a 1- to 5-star rating system. We'll cover that later in this chapter. Below that, you can view your photos in the folders that you put them in. If you put all of your photos into the Pictures folder, they'll be listed there. If you added your photos from another folder, they'll be listed in that folder. So, as you can see, Photo Gallery does a pretty darn good job of organizing your photos for you. Just the ability to see them by date is awesome. However, make sure you read on, because tags will seriously take your photo management to the next level.

What Tags Are and Why You Should Use Them

MATT KLOSKOWSKI

Tags are probably one of the easiest, yet most powerful ways to organize your photos. The best way to explain them is the printed-photos-in-a-box example. Let's say I sat down one day and decided to get organized. I'd take all of the photos in the box and separate them into piles. My son Ryan would get one pile, my son Justin another, maybe my wife would get a third. Photos from our trip to Japan would go into another pile, and other vacations would go into yet more piles. Then I'd wrap a rubber band around these photo piles or put them into an envelope and bask in the glory of my organized bliss. Now, when I want to see photos of Ryan, I can quickly open my box and find the Ryan pile. That's pretty much what tags let you do, but on the computer instead. You tag your photos based on the people, places, or events in them. So, I'd create a Ryan tag and associate all my photos of Ryan with that tag so I could easily find them later in Windows Photo Gallery. Tags, however, take organization to a whole new level. For example, what would I do if I took a photo of Ryan and Justin together? Which pile of photos would I put it in: Ryan's or Justin's? With a tag, it doesn't matter. I'd tag all photos of Ryan with his tag, no matter who else was in them, and do the same for Justin. Later, not only could I search for photos with the Ryan tag, but I also could search for photos that include both the Ryan and Justin tags. Then I'd get photos of them together. You see where we're going here? This tagging stuff really is cool, and will take your photo organization to a totally different level.

Creating and Using a New Tag

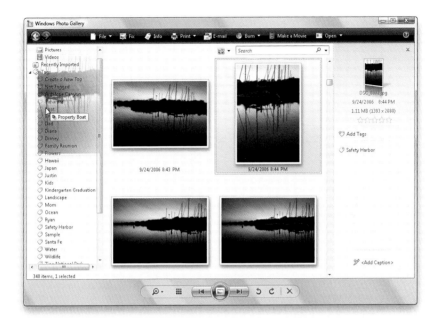

To create a new tag, in the Navigation pane along the left side of Windows Photo Gallery, click on the right-facing triangle next to Tags to expand it. Under Tags, click on Create a New Tag (the tag icon with a green plus sign), then type the name of the tag into the text field and hit Enter. You'll see your new tag appear in the list. Now, the tags don't do anything until you start using them. So, after you've imported your photos, find the photos that you want to associate with this new tag. For one photo, click on it. For more than one photo, Ctrl-click to select multiple photos. Once they're selected, click-and-drag the photo(s) over to the tag you want to associate them with on the left side. Release your mouse button when you hover over the tag, and it will now be assigned to the photo(s). If you want to see which tags are assigned to a photo, click the Info button in the top toolbar. You'll see the Info pane appear on the right (keep in mind, it may already be open). Then click on a photo and all of the photo's information (tags, size, date and time created, rating, and caption) will be displayed in that Info pane.

TIP

Here's my suggestion: tag your photos when you import them from your camera. Trust me, it'll only take a few minutes. If you wait until you have a few thousand photos to tag, the tagging process becomes darn near impossible. So make it part of your import process and get it done.

Finding Photos Using Tags

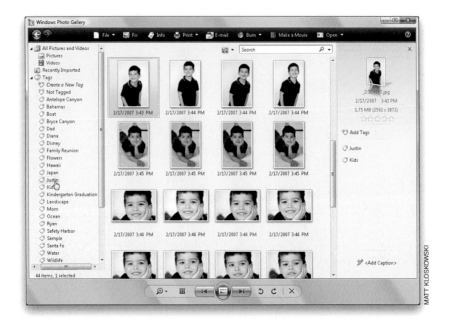

Now comes the cool part. You've tagged your photos, so you can start using them. For my example, I'm going to click on the All Pictures and Videos button at the very top of the Navigation pane on the left side of Windows Photo Gallery. This will show me everything in my photo library. At this point, I decide that I want to see the photos of my son Justin. Instead of scrolling through the thumbnails in the preview area to find them, all I've got to do now is click on the Justin tag in the Navigation pane. The preview area thumbnail view will change to show me only those photos that I've tagged with Justin—regardless of which folder they are in or the date the photos were taken. As long as I tagged any photos of Justin every time I imported them into the computer, they'll show up in this list. To get back to another view, simply click on All Pictures and Videos again or on any one of the other sections in the Navigation pane on the left.

TIP

You can also find your photos based on tags by typing the tag name in the Search field at the top right of the preview area.

Using Multiple Tags

Okay, the previous example was cool enough because now I have an easy way to find photos of my son Justin. But it gets better. Way better. Let's say that you've been very diligent about tagging photos when you import them to your computer. For me, I've not only been tagging Justin's photos, but I've been tagging my son Ryan and the rest of my family members, as well. So, I decide that I want to find all the photos of Ryan and Justin (two tags that I've created). Well, first I'd click on the Justin tag, just like in the previous tip. Then, Ctrl-click on the other tag you want to add to it—in this case Ryan. Now my center preview area will show me all photos tagged with Justin or Ryan. As you can imagine, as your photo library grows you could literally have hundreds, if not thousands, of photos of your kids. So you'll probably want to take this a step further. To find photos of Justin and Ryan that were taken on Halloween in 2005, under Date Taken, expand the 2005 year, then October, and Ctrl-click on Oct 31, Monday, too. Your list will contract to show only those photos from that specific date. That is powerful stuff, and it's a way of organizing your photos that you simply can't do by just putting them into folders on your computer.

Knowing What Type of Tags to Create

So, how do you know what type of tags to create? The possibilities are endless and your tag collection can get pretty unwieldy at some point. First, you'll want to create tags for the important people in your life. Probably not every single person you come into contact with, but at least the important people (family, close friends, and don't forget your pets). People are the single most important subject that we want to see when we search for our photos, so it makes sense to start there. You'll also want to create tags for important events. Not necessarily holidays or birthdays, because you have the Date Taken options to search for photos and you'd be doing duplicate work. Things like graduations, family reunions, bar mitzvahs, etc., all make great candidates because you'll likely forget the exact dates, but they're still important events. Vacations are another good example, but I'd categorize them as places—Bahamas, Hawaii, Disney, etc. In the end, it's up to you, but these are some examples that I've found work well at organizing your photos without getting to the point where you need to organize the way you've organized your photos.

TIP

You can create tags within tags, as well. Say you create a Flowers tag. Well, you can Right-click on the Flowers tag and choose Create Tag and start creating children of that tag—Daisies, Tulips, Sunflowers, etc.

Rating Your Photos and Picking the Keepers

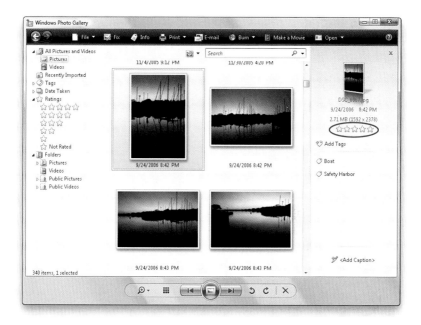

When you want to show people your photos, you can bet that the sure way to put them to sleep is to show them all 350 of your vacation photos (in fact, you can bet they'll be talking about you later). One thing I've found with digital is that people are taking more photos. It's cheaper and easier, so why not? However, most people (and I mean everyone besides you, the photographer) probably don't want to see all of them. You'll want a quick way to pull up your favorites so you can show the best ones. But, you don't want to delete the rest. They're still good photos; you just want to show off the very best. This is called sorting, and Windows Photo Gallery provides a good workflow for it: After you've imported your photos, and you see them in the center preview area, click on the first one and make your thumbnails large enough to see them well. Now, give a star rating to the best photos by pressing the numbers 1–5. That's probably easier said than done. How do you know what to rate the photos? Here's my suggestion:

★★★★★	These are the absolute best photos—the ones you'll print.
★★★★	These are good photos—ones you still want to show off, but probably won't be printed. This list will likely be larger than your 5-star list.
★–★★★	I don't use them. Do you really need five levels of ratings? It's either a photo I want to show off or it isn't. It gets too confusing to me to have all of the in-between photos. Think about it, what would you ever do with a 2-star rated photo?

Finding Your Favorites

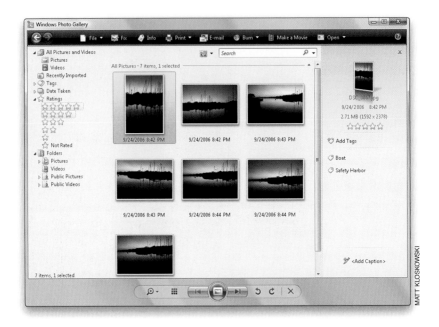

Now that you've gone through and rated your photos, you can show off your favorites to your friends easier. Obviously, you want them to see your 5-star rated photos because those were the absolute best. So, under the Ratings area, click on the 5-star button and you'll only see those photos. However, you really like the 4-star photos too, so you'll probably want to show them off as well. Just like with tags, Ctrl-click on the 4-star button to add those to the view. Now you can show off only your favorites and the whole experience will be better (and faster) for all of those viewing.

TIP

If you come across a photo that is flat-out horrible, there's no need to clutter your library. Delete it by pressing the red X button in the bottom toolbar, or by just pressing the Delete key.

Viewing Your Photos in a Slide Show

Now that you know how to rate and find your favorite photos, you'll want a cool way to show them off. Sure, you can open Windows Photo Gallery and show them there, but that's boring. You want to make an impact, and a slide show does just that. First things first: get your favorites onscreen by filtering so you only see your 4- and 5-star rated photos. Then, click on the Play Slide Show button at the bottom-center of the window (or press F11). This starts a slide show of your photos. What I like most about this is that it removes the distracting interface you see in Photo Gallery. If you're trying to show off a photo in Photo Gallery, the viewers' eyes are darting around to all of the different photos there. Plus, they're probably looking at the Fix pane and the other buttons and wondering to themselves (or asking you), "What does that do?" This way, you take all of the distractions away. Once in a slide show, you can use the controls at the bottom: To skip forward or go back, just click the Next or Previous buttons in that bar or press the Left or Right Arrow keys on your keyboard. To exit the slide show, click the Exit button or just hit the Esc key on your keyboard to get back to Photo Gallery.

The slide show controls at the bottom automatically hide themselves. If you don't see them at the bottom of the screen, just move your cursor around for a second and they'll appear.

TIP

Spicing Up Your Slide Show

Viewing your photos in a slide show is cool enough, but it gets better. First, click the Play Slide Show button at the bottom of the Windows Photo Gallery window to start playing a slide show. Once the slide show starts, look at the controls at the bottom of the screen. All the way over on the left you'll see a Themes button. Click on it to display a list of fade options and themes to help make your slide shows more visually interesting. At the top of the list are various ways to fade the images in your slide show from one photo to the next. Fade simply fades one photo out and another one in. Pan and Zoom (my personal favorite) will slowly pan across your photos and zoom in and out on them. This is a lot like the Ken Burns effect and really helps make your slide shows more interesting to watch. Finally, you can choose from various visual themes by clicking on one of the options on the bottom half of the list. Make sure you check these out because they do indeed take the "Wow!" factor of your slide shows (and photos in general) up a notch. (*Note:* The Windows Vista Home Basic edition includes only a limited number of themes.)

Changing the Way You View Your Photo Thumbnails

The way you see your photo thumbnails isn't set in stone. Sure you can change the thumbnail size using the Zoom button at the bottom of Windows Photo Gallery, but you can show some more information about your photos, as well. To change your view, click on the Choose a Thumbnail View button next to the Search field at the top right of the window. You'll see a pop-up menu with various ways to view and sort your photos in Photo Gallery. For example, to see the date and time that the photo was taken, choose Thumbnails with Text. To see the name of the file, the date and time it was taken, the size, ratings, and caption, choose Tiles. You can also change the way that Photo Gallery sorts your photos. By default, you're seeing the newest photos at the top and the oldest at the bottom. However, if you click on Sort By in this pop-up menu, you'll see there are options for sorting by file size, rating, and image size, among others.

Emailing a Photo

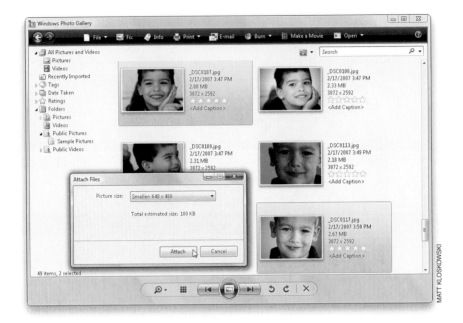

I know, I know. We covered emailing back in Chapter 6. However, one of my favorite little things about Windows Photo Gallery is the E-mail button in the top toolbar. It makes total sense. You're looking at your photos and you can see them visually, so what better place to give you the ability to email them to someone? To use it, just select the photo (or photos) that you want to email. Then click the E-mail button and the Attach Files dialog will pop open. Choose a Picture Size setting from the pop-up menu (if you're emailing them, it's best to keep this small—640x480 is a good setting) and click the Attach button. If your Windows Mail isn't already open, it will launch and create a brand new email for you. All you've got to do is fill in the To and Subject fields, write a message, and click Send.

Finding Out More Info About Your Photos (Metadata Definition)

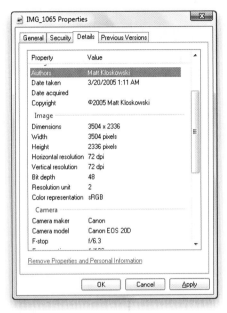

Whether you know it or not, each time you press the shutter on your camera to take a picture your camera automatically stores information about that photo. Things like the date it was taken, whether or not flash was used, the size of the photo and lots of other information is saved right into the picture itself (albeit hidden, so it doesn't actually show up on the photo when you look at it). All this stuff is called metadata, and that's basically just a techie term for information about your photo—in other words, file info. You can see the file info by clicking on the photo in Windows Photo Gallery and then clicking the Info button to open the Info pane (if it isn't already open). Heck, you can even change some of the information right there, like the filename, date, or even the title of the photo. However, there's a lot more file information available, and if you're the type that wants to see it, then Right-click on a photo and choose Properties. Here you'll find more information than you ever wanted to know about that photo. Things like the author (the person who took the photo), the camera make and model, and even copyright information are all readily available in this dialog. Just scroll down and you'll see that it's all categorized based on the type of information like Description, Origin, Image, Camera, and so on.

Changing File Info or Properties

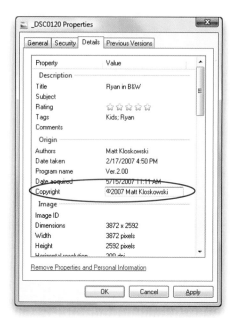

In the previous tip, I talked about viewing the file information (a.k.a. metadata) about your photos. Well, sometimes you may want to change that information, especially if you're sending these photos to other people. Plus, the more information you have about your photos, the more options you have to search for them later on. So, Right-click on a photo and choose Properties. Here you can add an author (whoever took the photo), the camera make and model, and even copyright information. Just hover over a Value field (to the right of the field name) and you'll see a text field or pop-up menu appear for the ones you can edit. Click on the field, type your text (or make a choice from the pop-up menu), and hit Enter, and that'll add to or change that field. As soon as you do this, that new information is automatically saved in your photo (again, not visibly, but behind the scenes) and will travel with it. That way, if you email it to someone or place it on the Web, whoever downloads the photo will be able to see the file info as well.

TIP

A copyright can be very important and can help protect you if you ever use your photos for commercial purposes. If you do, I'd select all of your photos at once (Ctrl-A), then Right-click on one of them and choose Properties. In the Copyright field, add your copyright information once (press Alt-0169 to get the copyright symbol) and it'll be added to all of your photos.

Ordering Prints Online

Gone are the days of dropping film off at your local store to be developed. In fact, gone are the days of dropping off a disc or memory card because now you can do it all online. Windows Photo Gallery has a feature that lets you send your photos to be printed right from within the program itself. First, select the photos that you want to print. Then click on the Print button in the top toolbar. Choose Order Prints from the pop-up menu. The first screen in the Order Prints dialog will ask you who you want to order prints from. For this example, I chose Shutterfly because I've used them before. After you pick a company, click the Send Pictures button. If you get a warning telling you that personal information may be included in your picture files, just turn on the Don't Show Again checkbox and press the Send button. The next screen you see lets you choose the quantity, size, and type of print that you want (you may have to log in first, depending on the company). After you make your choices, click Next to go through the checkout process, where you'll have to give your shipping information as well as a payment method (sorry, it ain't free). Within a few days, your prints will arrive at your door.

Printing to Your Printer

Once you've imported and fixed your photos, you're probably ready to see them on something else besides a computer screen. As great as computers and websites are these days, there's still nothing like seeing your photos printed on paper. So click on the photo (or photos) that you want to print, click on the Print button, and choose Print (or just click on the photo and press Ctrl-P). This opens the Print Pictures dialog. Here you have a few choices to make. First, choose your printer from the Printer pop-up menu. Then choose the paper size, quality (I usually set this to the highest available), and paper type (see the next three tips on getting good prints for more on these settings). Once you're done, click on Print and your photo will be sent to the printer.

TIP

When you go into the Print Pictures dialog, check out the right-hand side for some cool printing presets. There's everything from full-page photos to a template for printing wallet-sized photos. They're a huge timesaver, so make sure to check them out.

The Secret to Getting Good Prints, Part 1

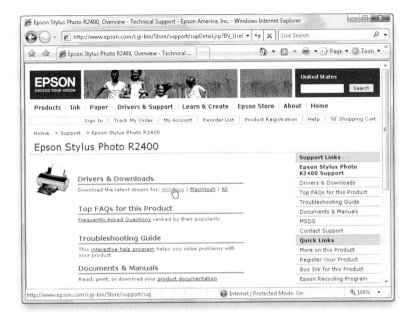

Ever print something out and it looks nothing like what you saw onscreen? Trust me, you're not alone. This happens all the time, but there are some ways to help avoid it. First, make sure you download software updates for your printer. See, when you install your printer on your computer, you install software drivers. This is how your printer communicates with your computer. You should check the printer vendor's website every so often to see if there are any updated drivers for your printer.

The Secret to Getting Good Prints, Part 2

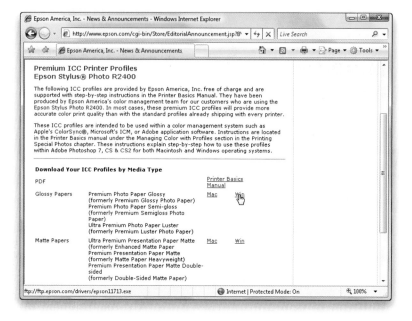

Okay, I'm going to warn you now: this one gets a little tricky. One area that's very important to printing is the paper. Most people go out and buy the cheapest paper they can find. If you're on a tight budget, I totally understand and that's fine. But just know that you're not going to get the print quality that you want. Your best bet, if you want a great print, is to buy the paper that goes with your printer. For example, if you have an Epson printer, then buy the Epson paper. Now, once you buy that paper, you need to go to the manufacturer's website and download the printer (ICC) profiles for that exact paper. I know it sounds like a lot of work, but remember, you're reading this because you're not happy with your prints. Fortunately, printer manufacturers' websites usually have an area dedicated to downloads and support. Once you're there, do a search (they also usually have a search field) for your paper's profile. In my case, I did a search for "Epson R2400 Ultra Premium Luster ICC" since I have the Epson R2400 and I'm using Epson's Ultra Premium Photo Paper Luster. In your case, substitute the "Epson R2400" part with your printer and the "Ultra Premium Luster" part with the type of paper you buy. Once you find the Windows profile for your paper, download and install it on your computer.

The Secret to Getting Good Prints, Part 3

Okay, last step. Once you download and install the profile for your exact paper, you're ready to print, so click on the Print button in Windows Photo Gallery and choose Print. The Print Pictures dialog opens. Choose your printer from the Printer pop-up menu and then choose the paper size that you bought. Next, under Quality, choose the highest quality option there is to offer. They are usually listed from highest to lowest, so the highest option will be at the top of the list. Finally, and this is very important, under Paper Type make sure you choose the exact paper type that you bought and installed the ICC profile for. Now you're ready to click Print and sit back and wait for your great-looking print to come out. Whew! I know it's a lot, but seeing that killer print makes it all worth it. Plus, in the end you really only have to do this once. From now on, you've got everything you need and you're good to go for the next time.

CHAPTER EIGHT

Music

Play and Organize Music with Windows Media Player

It seems like everyone is listening to music on their computers these days. I've got to admit that I rarely listen to CDs anymore. Most of the music I listen to all the time is loaded on my laptop, and I can get to it any time I want without lugging around a CD case. What makes this possible is a program called Windows Media Player. It's not new to Windows Vista, as Windows XP had Media Player, as well, but there is a brand new version of it in Vista. Overall it's the same program, but there are brand new features specifically for Vista. So if you've never used Media Player before, then read on. Even if you have, I bet you'll pick up a few tips on how to get the most out of the new version.

Add Files to Your Library

There are several ways to add media items to Windows Media Player's library. The most useful is to monitor or search certain folders on your hard drive for added, moved, or new files. By default, Media Player monitors your personal folders (Music, Pictures, and Videos) and the similar Public folders, but you can change these settings at any time. To view the folders that Media Player is monitoring, click on the down-facing arrow beneath Library on the menu bar and choose Add To Library. Next, click the Advanced Options button to view the folders that are currently monitored. Use the Add To Library dialog to add, remove, or simply ignore folders. Click OK when you're finished. Media Player will now monitor only the folders that you've selected.

Another way to add files is by ripping them from an audio CD. When you insert an audio CD into your computer's CD drive and play it using Media Player, you'll be prompted to rip the tracks to your library. Basically, ripping a CD copies the CD's files to your computer's hard drive and lists them in Media Player's library. It's a great way to add your existing music to Media Player.

You can also download music and videos from online stores. Media Player offers several online stores where you can purchase and download digital media files directly to your computer. To view available online stores, click on the down-facing arrow beneath Media Guide on the menu bar and choose Browse All Online Stores, then choose from the services listed. Any purchased or downloaded media files from an online store will automatically appear in Media Player's library.

Create Playlists

Playlists in Windows Media Player are essential for organizing your digital media files. A playlist is a collection of your media files, and can contain any combination of music, video, or picture files. Organizing your media files in playlists helps you quickly sort, find, view, burn, or even sync your files with portable devices. To create a playlist, drag-and-drop items from the center Details pane onto the List pane on the right (as shown here; if you don't see the List pane, click on the Show List Pane button to the right of the Search field). Once you've finished adding files to your playlist, click the Save Playlist button at the bottom right, type a name for your new playlist, and press Enter on your keyboard. Your new playlist now appears under Playlists in the Navigation pane on the left. To play your playlist, select it in the Navigation pane and click the Play button at the bottom. To edit your playlist, Right-click on its name in the Navigation pane and select Edit in List Pane from the contextual menu. Now, make any changes you'd like, then click Save Playlist. To remove a playlist, Right-click on it in the Navigation pane and select Delete from the contextual menu.

TIP

You can quickly arrange items in a playlist by simply dragging-and-dropping them into any order you'd like. To do this, Right-click on any playlist in the Navigation pane and select Edit in List Pane. Next, rearrange your media files in the List pane, and then click Save Playlist when finished.

Create Auto Playlists

Another type of playlist is an auto playlist. Auto playlists are lists that automatically update using the criteria you specify when creating the playlist. For example, you may want to create an auto playlist of all music files added to your library within the last 30 days. This auto playlist would continuously update itself to display music files added to your library within the last 30 days only. This is an extremely powerful feature, and really allows you to customize your playlists in very intuitive ways. To create an auto playlist, Right-click on Playlists in the Navigation pane and select Create Auto Playlist from the contextual menu. Next, using the New Auto Playlist dialog, name your playlist and specify the criteria for it by clicking on the green + (plus sign) buttons and choosing them from the pop-up menus, then click OK when finished. Your new auto playlist will appear under Playlists in the Navigation pane.

View Media in Your Library

Windows Media Player does a nice job of organizing your media according to the type of files you place in your library. Media Player easily distinguishes your music, pictures, video, and other files from one another and places them together in the proper location. To quickly view your various media files, click on the Select a Category button at the left end of the Address Bar and choose a category (media type) to view. You can then sort your files for different views by selecting a view option under Library in the Navigation pane. The view options will vary depending on the media type selected (such as Artist, Album, Songs, Genre, etc., for music). Click through each view to discover new ways of sorting and viewing files in your library.

TIP

For even more browsing and sorting options, check out the additional views available for your libraries. To do this, Right-click on Library in the Navigation pane and select Show More Views from the contextual menu, or click on Library in the Address Bar and choose a view option there.

Find Items in Your Library

As you begin adding more and more media files to your library, it becomes more and more difficult to locate individual files. Fortunately, Media Player is designed to not only handle a very large number of files, but also to help you quickly locate them. To search for files in your library, click the Select a Category button on the Address Bar and select the type of file to search for from the pop-up menu. Then, type a name, description, or keyword in the Search field, and the results are displayed in the center Details pane. To clear your search results, click the Clear Search (X) button at the right end of the Search field.

TIP

To view the location of a file on your hard drive, Right-click on any file listed in the Details pane and select Open File Location from the contextual menu. This opens Windows Explorer and displays the exact location of the file on your hard drive.

Playing Your Music

You'd think this would be obvious, and it is. To play a file in Media Player, simply select any file listed in the Details pane under Library, click the Play button, and the file
begins to play. Easy enough! But, as with most things in life, there's always more than
one way to do something. You can also double-click the same file in the Details pane
to instantly begin playing the file. If double-clicking isn't your thing, then try Right-
clicking on the file in the Details pane and choosing Play from the contextual menu,
and you guessed it, your file begins playing instantly. There are probably other ways
to kick-start your files, but I don't want to overwhelm you with too many options.
We'll just take this nice and slow.

Rip a CD

Ripping an audio CD is an essential task in Media Player. The term "ripping" basically means copying the files from a CD to your computer's hard drive. It's how you add your existing music CDs, and your friends' CDs (just kidding, that would be illegal), to Media Player's library. To rip an audio CD, insert the disc into your computer's CD drive and open Media Player (if it doesn't launch automatically), then click Rip on the menu bar. You'll see all of the tracks on your CD listed. By default, all the tracks will be selected to be ripped. However, you can select which tracks will be ripped by turning on or off the checkboxes before each track. Once Media Player has begun ripping your CD, you can stop the process at any time by clicking Stop Rip near the bottom right of the window. Once the files have been ripped, they appear in your library.

TIP

By default, ripped CD audio tracks are converted and copied as Windows Media Audio (WMA) files, but you can change Media Player's rip settings. To have all ripped audio files converted to MP3s instead, click on the down-facing arrow beneath Rip on the menu bar, and choose Format>MP3. To view even more rip options, such as format, audio quality, etc., choose More Options from the Rip menu.

Burn an Audio CD

Burning CDs of your favorite music is probably the most common use for Media Player, other than playing your music files, of course, and fortunately, Media Player makes this task very quick and easy. To burn a CD of your favorite music, first make certain that Music is your selected category, then select the Songs view or a playlist in the Navigation pane. Next, click Burn on the menu bar. Now, simply drag-and-drop files from the Details pane to the Burn List on the right or simply click on the Burn "Playlist Name" link in the Burn List. Once you've finished building your list and you're ready to burn your CD, click Start Burn at the bottom right. If you have not already placed a blank CD-R/CD-RW disc in your CD drive, Media Player will prompt you to insert one. Once the disc is recognized, Media Player will begin burning your audio disc. By default, once the disc has been burned, it will automatically eject. (*Note:* You must have a CD drive capable of writing to CD-R/CD-RW media installed on your computer to burn audio CDs using Media Player.)

Sync Music with Portable Devices

You have a couple of options when it comes to syncing (copying) your music files to a portable music player. You can use Media Player to either sync your files automatically or manually. When you connect a device for the first time, Media Player will choose the sync option that works best for your music player and the size of your Media Player's music library. For example, if you have enough storage capacity on your portable device, Media Player will attempt to sync your entire music library. Then, each time that you connect your device in the future, Media Player will automatically update your device to match your library. If your library is larger than the storage capacity of your device, then Media Player selects manual sync. Manual sync allows you to choose which files or playlists are copied to your music player. After your device is set up for the first time, you'll be able to choose between automatic or manual sync at any time. To sync your portable music player, open Media Player, then connect your device to your computer. If you're prompted, select to sync your device using Media Player. Then, depending on the type of device and the setup of your library, you'll be given the option to sync automatically or manually. Make your choice and click Finish to begin syncing your device.

Sharing Music and Other Media

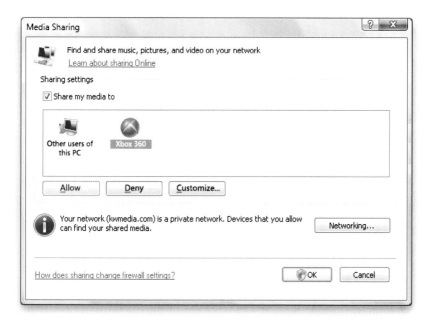

Sharing your media files is one of the coolest features of Media Player. If your computer is set up on a network, then you're able to share your library with other people's computers and other networked devices. You can share your music files, pictures, and videos. In my home, I have one dedicated media server where I store all of our music, photos, and videos and then stream them to other computers and devices (like the Xbox 360) located on my home network. This is perfect for keeping your files organized and easy for everyone to locate and access. To share your media files over a network, open Media Player, and from the Library button's pop-up menu, choose Media Sharing. In the Media Sharing dialog, turn on the checkbox for Share My Media, then, if you have devices connected, select the ones you want to share your files with in the field below, and click Allow. Click OK, and now your computer's Media Player shared files will appear on the allowed networked computers and devices. To stop sharing your files, select a device, click Deny, then click OK.

TIP

To find media that others on your network are sharing, go to the Media Sharing dialog mentioned above and turn on the checkbox for Find Media That Others Are Sharing, then click OK. The shared libraries now appear in Media Player under Library.

Customize the Look of Media Player

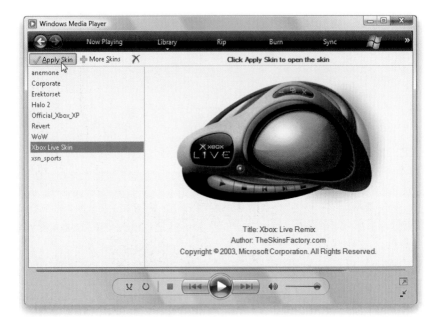

Media Player offers two views: Full mode and Skin mode. Full mode is Media Player in all its glory, displaying all of its features, navigation panes, library options, and full menu of player options. Full mode is the default view for Media Player. Skin mode makes Media Player a bit more compact, displaying the preview window and player controls. Press Ctrl-2 to switch to Skin mode, and press Ctrl-1 to switch back to Full mode.

The really cool thing about Skin mode is that you can change the look of Media Player to suit your own tastes. Try this: Press Ctrl-2 to switch to Skin mode, then click View>Skin Chooser from the menu bar. Now select a new skin for your player from the available options on the left and click Apply Skin when finished. You've got a new skin!

TIP

There are literally hundreds of skins available for Media Player. To choose a perfect skin for your player, click the More Skins button while in Skin Chooser. This will launch your Web browser and take you to Microsoft's webpage of Skins for Windows Media Player. Find just the right skin and download it for free.

Using Media Player's Enhancements

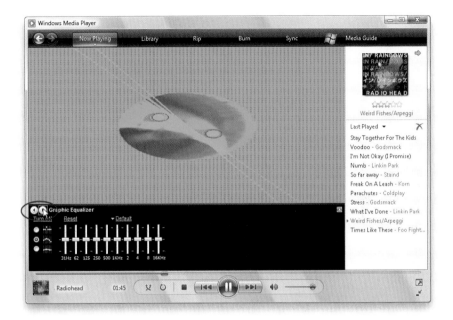

Media Player gives you far more control over your music and other media files than you might first think, and it does more than just play music. Using Media Player's enhancements, you can control cross-fading, apply volume leveling, adjust the equalizer for various music genres, tweak your video settings, and more. To view Media Player's enhancements, click on the down-facing arrow beneath Now Playing on the menu bar and choose Enhancements>Show Enhancements. The enhancements appear at the bottom of the player window. Click the left and right arrow buttons in the top left of the Enhancements pane to quickly change enhancements. To hide the settings, click the Close button (X) in the top-right corner of the Enhancements pane.

Changing Visualizations

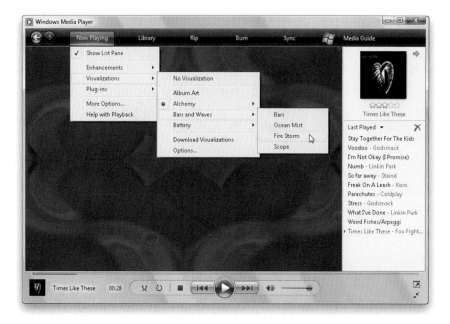

Media Player comes with a massive variety of visualizations for your music. Visualizations are a display of colors and shapes that move to the music as it's played. Visualizations can either be extremely relaxing or bring on a seizure that puts you in the fetal
position. Either way, they're cool! To turn on your visualizations, go under the Now
Playing button's menu and choose Visualization. Now, select a new visualization and it
appears in the Media Player window. To stop using visualizations, go back to the Now
Playing button's menu and choose Visualizations>No Visualizations.

TIP

To quickly change the visualization, Right-click anywhere on the Media Player
window and select a new visualization from the contextual menu.

Listen to Radio Stations

Bored with your library of music? Then check out Internet radio. Media Player offers a ton of Internet radio stations for just about every genre imaginable. To listen to Internet radio, click the Media Guide button. (If you browsed all the online stores, this may have changed to an Online Stores button. If so, go to the button's menu and choose Media Guide.) Click on the Internet Radio link in the box at the top right, and begin perusing the offerings from WindowsMedia.com. Select a genre, search using keywords, or select a featured station. (*Note:* Internet radio requires an active broadband connection to the Internet.)

Using Mini Player

We all love Media Player, but it's a bit large to leave open on your desktop all the time. Microsoft knew this, so they provided a way to use Media Player and not have it take up a single pixel of space on your desktop. To use Media Player's mini-player, Right-click on any open area of your Taskbar and choose Toolbars>Windows Media Player. Now when you minimize Media Player, it becomes a mini-player on the Taskbar, complete with player controls and a preview window if you hover over it with your cursor. To view video or visualizations, click the Show Video and Visualization Window button at the top right of the mini-player. Click the button again to turn off the window.

TIP

If you still want Media Player on your desktop, but smaller, click the Switch to Compact Mode button in the bottom right of the full-size player. To return to Full mode, click the same button again.

CHAPTER NINE

DVDs, Videos, and Making Movies
Making Your Family Superstars

Photos are one thing. They're easy enough to get off of your camera and onto your computer. Video is a whole different ball game, though. While it's easy enough to import videos to your computer, the editing and sharing process is a little different than what we're normally used to. In this chapter, we'll take a look at everything from how to get video from your camera to your computer, all the way to how to make that video look better by trimming, and adding transitions, music, and narration. Finally, we'll close with some ways in which you can share the video, so your family and friends can see it.

Getting Started: Import Video from Your Digital Camcorder

First things first: Before you can begin editing your next cinematic masterpiece using Windows Movie Maker, you have to get your video into your computer. Having the right hardware will make all of your projects far easier and less time-consuming when importing video. If you have an IEEE 1394 connection card or high-speed USB 2 connection available on your computer, then simply connect your digital camcorder to your computer using the included cable and you're done. Now, turn your camcorder on and set it to Play or View (this option may vary on your camcorder—you'll want to set your camcorder to playback mode). Autoplay will automatically recognize your camcorder, so click Import Video and follow the prompts to begin importing your video. You can also import by opening Windows Movie Maker (by clicking Start>All Programs>Windows Movie Maker). Choose File>Import from Digital Video Camera or select From Digital Video Camera in the Tasks pane on the left. Using the import dialog, name your file, choose a location to save your video file, select your video format, and click Next. Choose Import the Entire Video to my Computer and click Next. Movie Maker will rewind your video to its beginning, if necessary, and begin importing your video. When finished, your video file will be imported and ready for editing in Movie Maker.

Add the Essentials: Audio, Video, and Pictures

Movie Maker allows many different file types to be imported for use with your video projects. You can import a wide variety of video, picture, and audio files. These file types can be used in Movie Maker:

Video: .wmv, .mpeg, .m1v, .mp2, .mp2v, .mpe, .mpg, .mpv2, .wm, .asf, .avi, .dvr-ms

Pictures: .jpe, .jpeg, .jpg, .bmp, .gif, .jfif, .png, .tif, .tiff, .wmf, .dib, .emf

Audio: .wav, .wma, .mp2, .mp3, .mpa, .snd, .aif, .aifc, .aiff .asf, .au

Note: Other file types may be imported into Movie Maker, but may not be recognized or useable.

To add files for use with your video projects, choose File>Import Media Items or click on the Import Media button at the top left of the window. Select the files you wish to import by browsing your folders located in the Favorite Links pane of the Import Media Items dialog or click on Folders at the bottom to view more options. Browse your hard drive to locate and select your files, then click Import. The files appear in Movie Maker's Contents pane under Imported Media.

TIP

To select several files from a single location for import, Ctrl-click on each file you want to select, then click Import. You can also select multiple files by clicking on the first file in your list then Shift-clicking on the last file in your list. Or, you can simply drag-and-drop any file onto the Imported Media Contents pane.

Create and Save Your Project

By adding your video, music, and picture files to Windows Movie Maker, you've essentially created a project. A project in Movie Maker is a collection of files used to create your movie. And a project stores the information on your storyboard and timeline, including titles, credits, transitions, and effects. Once you've imported the files for your project, choose File>Save Project As, click on Browse Folders to pick a location on your hard drive to save your project, type in a filename, then click Save. To open a saved Project, choose File>Open Project, navigate to your saved Movie Maker project, select the project, and then click Open. You can also create a new project by choosing File>New Project.

TIP

To save time searching for the project you last worked on, you can set up Movie Maker to automatically open the last project worked on by choosing Tools>Options, then clicking on the General tab, turning on the checkbox for Open Last Project on Startup, and clicking OK. Now, each time you launch Movie Maker it will open the last project worked on.

It All Happens Here (Using the Storyboard)

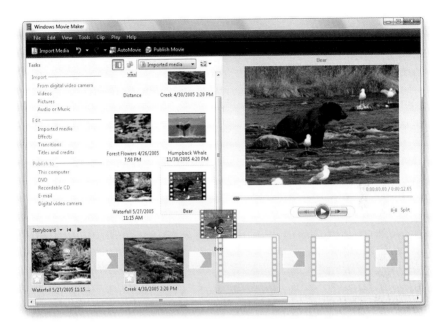

The Storyboard view at the bottom of Movie Maker is where it all comes together. You begin creating your movie by simply dragging-and-dropping your video and picture files from the Imported Media Contents pane onto the storyboard in the order (from left to right) that you want them to appear in your movie. To do this, select the file that you want to appear first in your movie and drag-and-drop it onto the first media clip icon on the storyboard. Continue dragging-and-dropping your files onto the storyboard until you have completed your movie.

TIP

You can easily rearrange your clips on the storyboard by dragging-and-dropping them into any order you'd like. So, if you decide the last video clip on the storyboard would work better at the beginning, simply drag-and-drop the last video clip in front of the first one on the storyboard. You can do this as many times as you'd like to get your movie just right.

Timing Is Everything (Trim Your Clips)

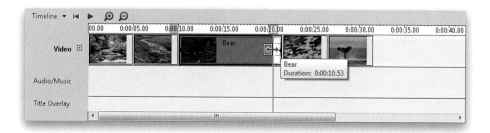

Inevitably, you're going to have portions of video clips that you either don't want to use or that you don't want seen in your final movie. You may have recorded the first five minutes of your daughter's birthday with the lens cap on your camcorder. While this is actually pretty funny, a five-minute blackout at the start of your movie probably isn't what your audience is hoping for. Unfortunately, I know this. Well, you can hide your shame by trimming it away. Movie Maker allows you to set a start trim point (where you want the clip to begin to play) and an end trim point (where you want the clip to end) for any clips on your timeline. To set trim points for your clips, go to your movie's timeline by choosing View>Timeline, then on the timeline, select the clip that you want to trim by clicking on it. Next, use the clip's trim handles to set your start and stop points. Trim handles appear as small, black triangles at the beginning and end of each clip. To set the beginning trim point, click-and-drag the beginning trim handle to the right, to any point on the clip's timeline, and let go. This sets your beginning trim point. You can view your exact location within the clip in the preview monitor on the right. Repeat the same steps to set the end trim point for your clip (click-and-drag the end trim handle to the left). To clear trim points from a clip, choose Clip>Clear Trim Points and you're right back where you started.

Splitting Up Is Easy to Do (Split Your Clips)

Some clips may just be too long, or maybe you'd like to insert a still picture or transition in the middle of a clip. Or, maybe even place a part of the first clip at the end of your movie. Well, fortunately for you, you can. Movie Maker allows you to split a clip as many times as you'd like. To split a clip, first select the clip you want to split by clicking on it in the storyboard or timeline. Next, click-and-drag the slider under the image in the pre-view monitor to the location where you want to split your clip and let go. Now, click the Split button to the right of the preview controls. Your clip is now split exactly where you indicated and appears on the storyboard and timeline as a new clip. You can now add a transition or reposition the clip anywhere on the storyboard.

There may also be times when you want to combine clips, and it only makes sense that if you can split 'em you can combine 'em. To combine clips, you have to select contiguous clips on the storyboard or timeline by Ctrl-clicking on each clip. Once you've selected the clips to be combined, choose Clip>Combine.

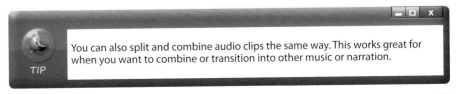

TIP

You can also split and combine audio clips the same way. This works great for when you want to combine or transition into other music or narration.

Be a Showoff (Add Transitions)

Without transitions, your clips would simply all run together without any break in the action. It is hard to tell a story without occasional pauses or indicating to your audience that the action, mood, location, time, etc., has changed. Transitions are a great way to convey this type of necessary effect. To add transitions between your clips, first select Transitions from the pop-up menu in the Contents pane, then drag-and-drop any of the available transitions onto any transition icon on the storyboard. You just added a transition between two clips. To preview your transition, select the clip before the inserted transition and click Play in the preview monitor. If you want a different transition, simply drag-and-drop a new one onto the transition icon and it replaces the previous transition. You can also delete any transition by Right-clicking on the icon on the storyboard and selecting Remove from the contextual menu.

TIP

To change the duration of a transition, go to the timeline by choosing View> Timeline, and click on the plus sign next to the Video track to expand it. Select the transition by clicking on it in the timeline. Next, drag the timeline towards the beginning or end of the clip, depending on whether you want to shorten or lengthen the transition's effect.

They're Not Just Effects, They're Special Effects

If you haven't noticed by now, Movie Maker is a powerful application for creating great movies, but it becomes even more versatile with the introduction of effects. The special effects in Movie Maker are perfect for adding just the right touch to your clips. Perhaps you're showing video of your grandparents to your little guys or making fun of someone's 40th birthday (not that any of you would ever do that). Well, if that's the case, try adding the Film Age, Oldest special effect to your video clip for that turn-of-the-century feel. To add special effects to any clip, select Effects from the pop-up menu in the Contents pane, then drag-and-drop any effect directly onto a clip where you want the special effect to appear. The Effect icon (the small star) in the bottom-left corner of the clip on the storyboard will darken, indicting that the clip has a special effect applied to it. To preview the effect, select the clip in the storyboard or timeline and click Play in the preview monitor. To delete an effect, Right-click on the Effect icon on the clip and select Remove Effects from the contextual menu.

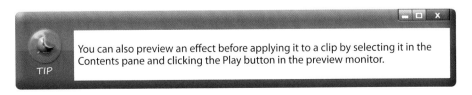

TIP

You can also preview an effect before applying it to a clip by selecting it in the Contents pane and clicking the Play button in the preview monitor.

Get Geeky with It (Add Narration)

Okay, showing a video to your wife's family of you wearing a woman's evening gown, complete with gloves and a tiara, may require a little explanation (and I hope it's a good one). Well, you can hopefully explain away one of your life's proudest moments by adding a little narration to your movie. To add narration to your movie (as I'm doing here to a vacation video), first select the location on your movie's timeline where you want to begin your narration by dragging the timeline slider to any point in your movie and letting go. This marks the spot in your video where your narration will be initially inserted. Next, choose Tools>Narrate Timeline, then click the Start Narration button, and speak into your microphone to begin recording. When finished, click the Stop Narration button. You'll be prompted to save your narration, so provide a filename for your narration, and click Save in the Save Windows Media File dialog. The narration file is automatically imported into your current project contents and placed on the Audio/ Music track of the timeline where you first began your narration.

Add Music

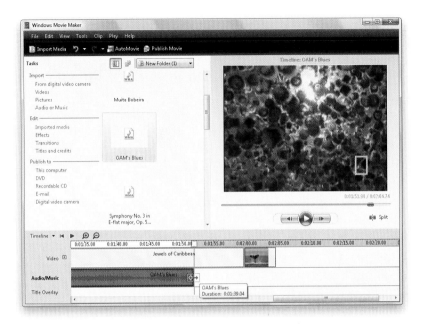

Another great way to add emotion to your movies is by using music to set a mood or to add a sense of drama or excitement. Movie Maker makes it incredibly easy to add music tracks to your video. You add music in the same way you add video clips, photos, or other media items: simply drag-and-drop music clips from your Contents pane Imported Media or Project folders onto the timeline. (*Note:* You can only add music clips in the Timeline view.) To add music files to your movie, first locate the position within your movie to insert the music file by dragging the timeline slider to the location you wish to insert the file and let go. Now drag-and-drop the music file onto the Audio/Music timeline, and it appears exactly where you indicated with the timeline slider. You can also position the music file anywhere on the Audio/Music timeline by simply dragging it to any location on the timeline. To trim your music file, drag either the left or right trim handle (the small, black triangles located at the ends of each clip) to trim either the beginning or end of the music file.

TIP

If you're adding music to a video clip that has sound, then mute the sound of your video clip so that only the music file is heard when playing. To do this, expand the Video track in the timeline, Right-click on the Audio track of any video clip that contains sound to be removed, and choose Mute from the contextual menu. Now, only the music you inserted will be heard during your movie.

Give Credit (Add Titles & Credits)

What's a movie without credits? Well, I don't know either, but it's not a movie. So, don't leave your audience wondering what they've just seen: add titles and credits to complete your movie. To insert a title for your movie, click on Titles and Credits under Edit in the Tasks pane, then click on Title at the Beginning and enter the text for your title. Next, click on Change the Title Animation and choose a title animation from the list that appears (click on one to see a preview), then click on Change the Text Font and Color, choose a font, color, transparency, size, and position, then click Add Title. Your movie title now appears at the beginning of your movie. To add credits, click on Titles and Credits in the Tasks pane once again, then click on Credits at the End. Type in your credits, change the text animation, font, and color, and click Add Title. (*Note:* When you type your credits, add them in the two-column section below the title line. Anything typed on a line in the left column will appear directly above what is then typed on that same line in the right column.) Your credits now appear at the end of your movie. You can also insert titles before a selected clip or insert a title overlay on any selected clip.

There Is an Easier Way: Use AutoMovie

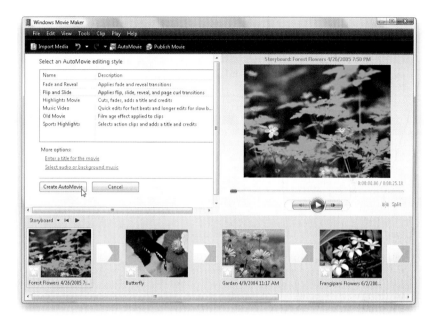

Now that I've shown you how to create your own movie by adding media items, transitions, special effects, music, narration, and credits, and how to put it all together, you should be able to produce a great movie in no time at all. However, you can skip all of this by simply clicking one button. I know, I should have started here, but where's the fun in that? For the lazy way out, once you've imported all of your media items and you're ready to create your movie, click the AutoMovie button at the top of the window. Next, select an AutoMovie editing style. Under More Options, enter a title and credits, and select any audio or background music, then click Create AutoMovie. Once AutoMovie has finished creating your movie, the media items appear on the storyboard/timeline. You can edit any portion of the timeline or simply publish your movie as is. It's just that simple.

Ready for Prime Time?
Preview Your Movie First

You've finished putting all of the pieces together and your movie appears to be complete, but before you publish your movie, be sure to preview it. You'll want to make certain that everything works exactly as you want it to and that the timing of transitions, music, and effects is just right. To preview your movie, select the first clip on the storyboard or timeline, then click the Play button in the preview monitor. Use the preview controls to stop, pause, and move forward and backward in your movie, if necessary, to locate and isolate potential problems. Once a problem is found, go to the storyboard or timeline and make any updates or changes, then preview the movie once again. Once all the issues have been resolved, it's time to publish your movie.

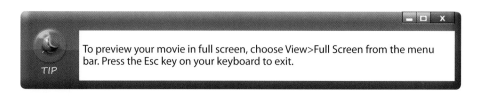
TIP
To preview your movie in full screen, choose View>Full Screen from the menu bar. Press the Esc key on your keyboard to exit.

Time to Share (Publish Your Movie)

The best part of creating your movie is the satisfaction of viewing the finished project. Whether you're creating a DVD, showing your movie on your home computer, or sending it to family and friends via email, it's a blast knowing that you created this little cinematic masterpiece. So, let the good times roll, it's time to publish your movie. When you're ready to share your movie with the world, or at least family and friends, click on the Publish Movie button at the top of the window. In the Publish Movie dialog, select where you want to publish your movie (your computer, a DVD, a CD, etc.), then click Next. Depending on your selection, you'll be prompted to insert a CD/DVD, name your movie, and so on. Once you've followed the prompts and your movie begins publishing, Movie Maker will display a progress bar showing the time remaining. When Movie Maker is finished publishing your movie, click Finish. Your movie is now ready to share. Enjoy!

CHAPTER TEN

Storing, Finding, and Viewing Your Files
Working with Files and Folders

Here's the chapter where we take a look at some of the nuts and bolts of the files on your computer. Not the system files that you don't care about, but your own files that you create (Word documents, photos, PDFs, spreadsheets, etc.). You'll learn how to use the brand new Instant Search feature, as well as how to set up your folders to make it easier to get to the files you want quickly. In general, you'll learn more about finding and viewing your files and everything about them, so if you're the geeky type, this one is for you.

Navigating Your Files and Folders (Windows Explorer)

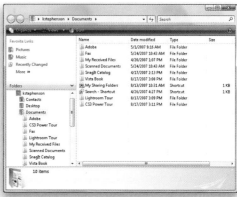

There's only one place in Windows Vista where you can view all of your files and folders at one time, and that's in Windows Explorer. Windows Explorer allows you to conveniently view, edit, move, and delete files on your computer. And it's a good thing, because without Windows Explorer it would be nearly impossible to manage your computer's files. To get to Windows Explorer, go to the Start menu, then click on All Programs>Accessories>Windows Explorer. By default, this will open Windows Explorer at your Documents folder. (*Note:* You can also get to the Documents folder by clicking on the Start menu, then clicking on Documents at the top right of the Start menu.) The Navigation pane on the left side of the window helps you locate your files and folders. In it, the Folders list displays your computer's file structure, where and how files and folders are stored, all users, and disc drives and hard drives. The Favorite Links are shortcuts to some of your favorite or most-used folders. Selecting any folder in the Favorite Links or Folders list instantly displays the items in the folder in the larger File list to the right. You can select, open, drag-and-drop, copy-and-paste, delete, or rename any file within Windows Explorer.

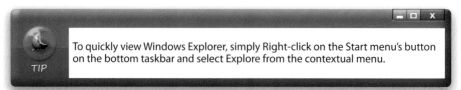

To quickly view Windows Explorer, simply Right-click on the Start menu's button on the bottom taskbar and select Explore from the contextual menu.

TIP

Customize Windows Explorer

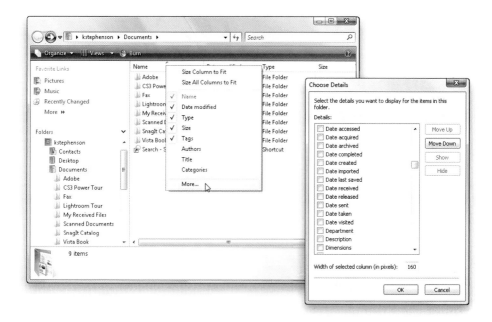

Now that you know how to view your computer's files using Windows Explorer, you'll probably want to make it look and work in a way that's best for you. No two computer users are
exactly the same, and how one person manages their files may not be the way that you'd
manage yours. So, Windows Explorer gives you the capability to customize how you view,
sort, and manage your files. To customize Windows Explorer, Right-click on any column
header in the File list on the right side of the window, then choose any available column,
or More from the contextual menu for an insane number of options. Inserting additional
columns gives you great flexibility to include the information that's important to you when
browsing your files. And now that you've added all the columns that you could possibly
ever need, you'll probably want to organize them in order of importance. To do this, simply
click on each column header and drag-and-drop them in any order that you'd like.

Getting Information About Your Files and Folders

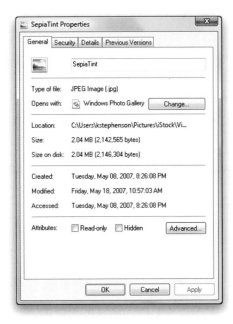

When was this picture taken? When did I create this file? How large are my files? These are all really good questions, and eventually you'll probably need to know their answers. You can quickly view any file's or folder's information by Right-clicking on the file and selecting Properties from the contextual menu. This opens the file's Properties dialog. The General tab tells you the location of your file, type of file, its size, and gives you the dates that the file was created, modified, and last accessed. You can click the Security, Details, and Previous Versions tabs for even more information. You can even assign certain attributes to your files or, in some cases, add your own custom properties.

TIP

For a quick view of a file's basic details, simply select (click on) a file in any open Explorer window. When a file is selected, some of its available properties appear at the bottom of the window. However, for more detailed properties you'll still want to open the file's Properties dialog.

Create and Delete Files and Folders

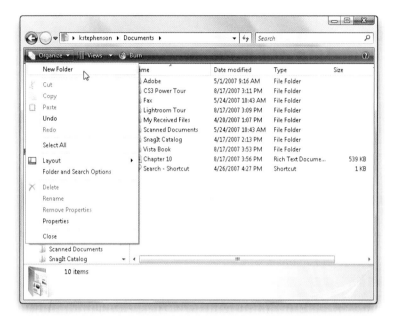

Now that you're becoming an expert at navigating your computer, you'll want to start creating your own folders and files. Fortunately, Windows Vista makes this crazy easy. To create a new folder, click on the Organize button at the top left of your Windows Explorer window and select New Folder from the pop-up menu. This will create a new folder in the File list of wherever you're browsing (here, I'm in my Documents folder, so the new folder will be in the Documents folder). See? It's simple! Now you can start storing files in your new folder. To populate your new folder, simply copy-and-paste, drag-and-drop, or save any number of files to your new folder. Creating folders is a great way to keep track of and organize your files. To delete files and folders, you have several options. You can drag-and-drop files or folders onto the Recycle Bin on your desktop, select (click or Ctrl-click on) the file(s) or folder(s) that you want to delete and then press the Backspace key or the Delete key on your keyboard, or Right-click on any file or folder and select Delete from the contextual menu.

TIP

You can also create a new folder by Right-clicking in any blank space in a Windows Explorer File list and selecting New>Folder from the contextual menu.

Customize Your Folders

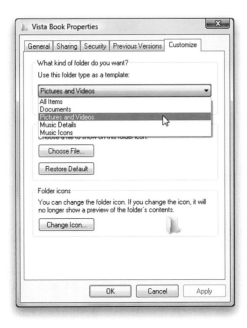

Another great feature of Windows Vista is the ability to customize your folders. Not all folders are the same. You'll probably have folders that hold very different types of files. If you're like me (and you probably are), your folders will contain movies, music, pictures, documents, or any combination of files. Windows Vista makes it very easy to manage these types of folders. To customize your folders, Right-click on any folder and select Properties from the contextual menu. This opens the folder's Properties dialog. Next, click the Customize tab. Here you can tell Windows how it should best interpret the contents of your folder, and how the contents should be displayed. At the top of the dialog, click on the pop-up menu for Use This Folder Type as a Template to select an appropriate template for your folder. For instance, selecting Pictures and Videos will display medium-sized thumbnails of any pictures or video clips contained in the folder. This makes it very easy to identify individual files. Or, when selecting Documents, you're given a Details view of your files. So, select the most appropriate folder template for easy viewing.

Rename Files and Folders

Renaming your files may sound like an easy task, and it is if you know how to do it, but if you don't, you'd swear Windows was out to get you. Things don't always have to be obvious to be simple. To rename any file or folder, Right-click on the file's name or icon and select Rename from the contextual menu. This will highlight the filename. Now you're able to rename your file to anything that you'd like—just start typing. When you're finished, press Enter on your keyboard or deselect the file by clicking anywhere outside the filename text field.

TIP

If you mess up while renaming your file, you don't have to start over. Press the Esc key on your keyboard and your file returns to its original name.

Move and Copy Your Files and Folders

It's inevitable, eventually you're gonna have to move things around in Windows Vista. Fortunately, organizing your files and folders is as simple as dragging-and-dropping them wherever you'd like. To move a file, click-and-hold on the file's icon or name, and drag-and-drop it to its new location (a new folder, the desktop, an external hard drive, etc.). Files can be moved to just about anywhere, and as many times as you'd like, so go crazy. To copy a file to another location on your computer without using the drag-and-drop method, Right-click on the file's icon or name and select Copy from the contextual menu. Then, navigate to the location on your hard drive (or CD or external hard drive) where you want to place the copied file, Right-click on any blank area of the window showing that folder's or drive's contents, and select Paste from the contextual menu. The file is now copied to that location. You can also quickly paste your copied file to any folder by Right-clicking on the folder and selecting Paste from the contextual menu. This places a copy of your file in the folder without having to open the folder first.

Selecting Files and Folders

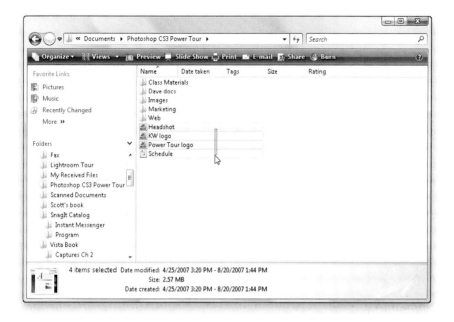

There are several ways to select files in Windows Vista, and you'll use different techniques depending on how many files you're selecting. To select a single file, simply click once on the file and it's now selected (if you have the Folder Options dialog, found under the Tools menu, set to Single-Click to Open an Item, hover over the file to select it). To select multiple files, press-and-hold the Ctrl key on your keyboard and click on each file that you wish to select. When selecting a concurrent group of files, click-and-hold your mouse button just to the right of the first file's filename, then drag your cursor over the additional files that you wish to select. Release the button and all the files are selected. To select all the files in a folder or open window, press Ctrl-A. To deselect your files, click on any blank space in the folder or open window, or on the desktop.

Change Folder Views

Folder views are very useful for working with and managing your files. And Windows Explorer's new scalable "live" icon feature for the folder views in Windows Vista is a huge improvement over the system icons in earlier versions of Windows. You're still able to display a folder's contents as Tiles, Details, List, and Small Icons, but try using the live icon slider to display a thumbnail of the actual content of your file. This makes identifying files much easier. Live icons display thumbnails of your photos, album art for music files, and the actual page layout and content of document files. To adjust your folder view, click the down-facing arrow next to the Views button at the top-left of any Windows Explorer window. Use the slider to customize the size of your icons, from small Tiles to Extra Large Icons, and everywhere in between.

Show and Hide Panes

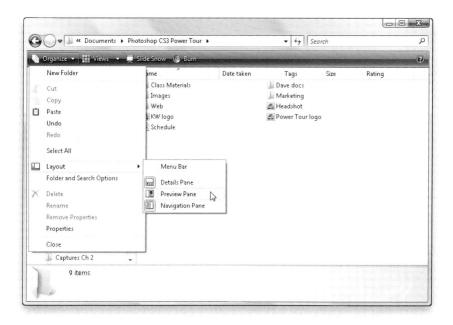

Using Windows Vista has made navigating your folders and browsing files extremely painless. Windows Explorer panes give you detailed file information, the location of files on your hard drive, and many additional options that allow you to work effectively from within any window. However, you may miss the old look of Windows (where you didn't have so much information to consider), or you may simply prefer a window that displays files only. You may also prefer to set up your windows differently than Vista's default layout. If this is the case for you, then you can turn the panes on or off or change a window's layout very quickly. To do this, click on the Organize button at the top left of any window, then choose Layout. Here you can select which panes to show or hide—hide 'em all, show only the ones you want, or show them all.

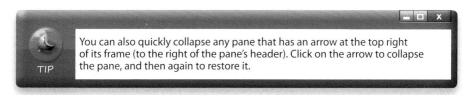

TIP

You can also quickly collapse any pane that has an arrow at the top right of its frame (to the right of the pane's header). Click on the arrow to collapse the pane, and then again to restore it.

Using the Address Bar

As with Windows XP, the address bar at the top left of any Windows Explorer window in Vista shows you exactly where the file or folder you're browsing is stored on your hard drive. But Vista has gone a step further and made the address bar a true navigation tool. The enhanced address bar allows you to quickly navigate forwards or backwards along an address (or navigation path). By clicking the arrow to the right of each folder in the navigation path, you can easily move to any location within the folder (or path). To use this feature, click an arrow to the right of a folder within the path in the address bar and then select a folder from the pop-up menu. This opens the new folder in the Explorer window that you're currently working in.

Instantly Search for Files

You can now get instant search results from just about any window or Vista application installed on your computer, which is extremely convenient. But what really makes Vista's Instant Search such a powerful feature is that it's contextual, which means that it performs a search based on your current activity. So, if you're searching a folder of Word documents, it gives the results of the files you're browsing. It's the same for music titles in Windows Media Player or applications in your Control Panel. You'll find Instant Search located in the top-right corner of most windows and applications throughout Windows Vista. To use Instant Search, just type a keyword, some text contained in the file, or all or part of the filename itself into the Instant Search field. As you type, results are displayed automatically (termed "fast-as-you-can-type" results). Once you've located the file you're searching for, simply double-click on the file to open it.

TIP

To use Instant Search to search your entire computer, go to the bottom of the Start menu and simply begin typing in the Instant Search field. The field is active anytime you open Vista's Start menu. Found results are instantly displayed above, where the program list was.

Using Advanced Search

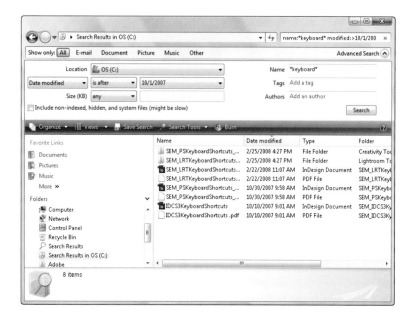

Sometimes finding the file you're looking for can be a bit tricky, especially if you can't quite remember where you last saved it, what you named it, or even the type of file you saved it as. Don't feel stupid—it happens to all of us. You may even want to find an entire group of files or a particular type of file that you have saved in various locations on your hard drive. Well, if you find yourself struggling to find the files you're looking for using Instant Search, try filtering your results using Windows Vista's Advanced Search. To perform your next power search, do this: Go to Start>Search (listed above Recent Items on the right side of the Start menu). Next, click the down-facing arrow next to Advanced Search at the top right of the Search window. This will display advanced filters. Use the filters to specify information about your search. When finished, click the Search button. Results are listed in the pane below. To view any found file, simply double-click the file's name to open it.

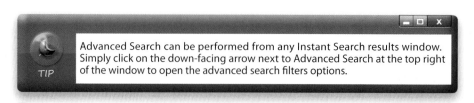

TIP

Advanced Search can be performed from any Instant Search results window. Simply click on the down-facing arrow next to Advanced Search at the top right of the window to open the advanced search filters options.

Sorting Files and Folders

Sorting your files gives you a very quick and convenient way of organizing the contents of any folder. Sorting files will list all items in a folder concurrently. For instance, if you sort by Name, your files will be listed in alphabetical order. Sort by Size and all items are sorted from smallest to largest. This can make locating files a breeze and helps to bring order to otherwise large and difficult to manage folders. To sort your files, Right-click on a blank space anywhere in the Contents pane of any open folder and under Sort By, choose a sort option. You can also click on any column header located at the top of the Contents pane to sort by that column. A small arrow will appear at the top of the header to let you know whether the column is sorting in ascending or descending order. By default, you can sort items by Name, Date Modified, Type, Size, and Tags. Be sure to try different column headers to see how each affects the arrangements of your files. What works for one folder of items may not work for the next.

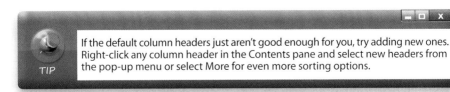

If the default column headers just aren't good enough for you, try adding new ones. Right-click any column header in the Contents pane and select new headers from the pop-up menu or select More for even more sorting options.

TIP

Grouping Files and Folders

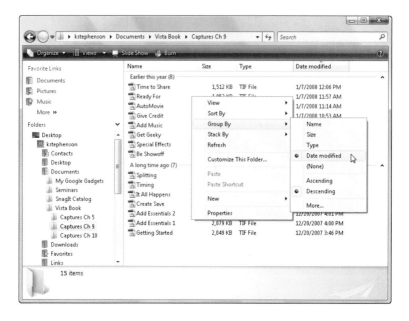

Grouping is one of two new views in Windows Vista for browsing a folder's contents and takes sorting one step further. While sorting does a great job of organizing all items in a folder based on your preferences, it doesn't provide a detailed overview of sorted files—grouping does. Try this: Right-click any blank space within your folder and select Group By>Date Modified. This organizes your files by the date each file was modified. This grouping displays recently modified files, files modified earlier in the year, and files modified last year. This makes identifying particular files within given timeframes much easier than sorting alone. You can group by different criteria depending on the file type (i.e., by ratings for image files).

Stacking Files

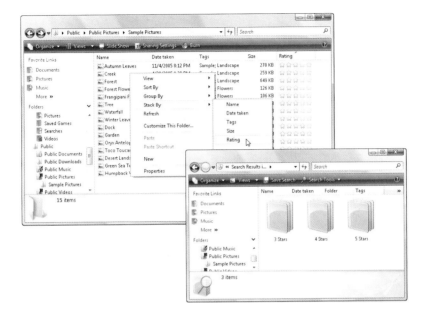

Stacking is the second new view introduced by Windows Vista that displays a folder's contents "stacked" by values in a specific column. With that said, stacking behaves very similarly to grouping; however, stacking places all of the sorted files in what are essentially virtual folders. They are virtual because they don't physically reside in any location on your hard drive. They only exist within your folder. You would double-click a stacked item to open and view its contents as you would any other folder. So, for large folders of items, stacking brings another level of organization not possible with earlier versions of Windows.

Restoring Files from the Recycle Bin

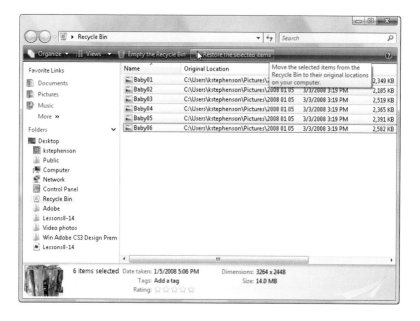

Okay, you've accidentally deleted the entire folder containing every picture of your child's birth, what do you do? You've got two choices here: (1) You can tell the wife and hope and pray that she remembers why she married you in the first place and spares your life. Or, (2) you go to your Recycle Bin and restore 'em. I recommend restoring the files to cover your enormous blunder and never speaking of it to anyone. To restore any deleted files, open your Recycle Bin by double-clicking on its icon on your desktop, select the folder and/or files located in the Contents pane that you want to restore, then click the Restore This Item button on the menu bar. This restores (places) the deleted items back to their previous location (where they were originally deleted from).

Changing an Icon

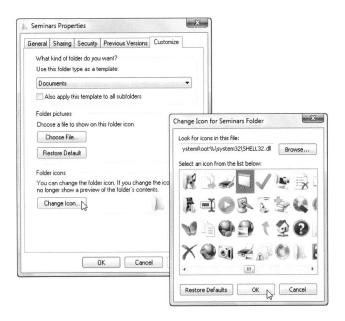

Customizing Windows Vista, or any operating system for that matter, is key to how you enjoy your computing experience. The first place that I always start is with my icons. I like to personalize my files, folders, and applications with icons that better identify what they are and what they contain, just because I prefer things my way. You can change virtually any icon on your computer by Right-clicking a folder, file, or application icon and selecting Properties from the contextual menu. Next, click on the Customize tab in the Properties dialog, and click the Change Icon button located under Folder Icons near the bottom of the dialog. Use the Change Icon dialog that appears to browse your hard drive for available icons (.ico files). Once you've selected a new icon, click the OK button and your new icon will instantly appear.

Managing Your Files and Folders the Vista Way

This is one of those tips that comes from personal experience. You know how Vista automatically creates Pictures, Videos, Downloads, Documents, Music, etc., folders for you? Well I used to just ignore these folders and create my own. For some reason, I didn't want anyone telling me where to store my stuff. However, over the last couple years I've changed. I realized (even in Windows XP) that those folders are actually a good thing. They help you work faster and easier. Why? Because of little things really. When you save your files, these folders are always readily accessible because that is where Vista wants you to save them. When you use the backup features in Vista, it can automatically back things up without you having to intervene and specify certain folders. And if you're ever moving your files from one computer to another, having the default folders is a lifesaver. In the end, it's just easier. Think about how many times you see these folders somewhere, especially if you haven't used them in the past. So if you're like me and ignored those folders in the past, give 'em a try. In the long run, I think you're really going to like them.

TIP

If you lose track of where these folders are, then finding them is a cinch. In Windows Explorer, as well as any Save or Open dialogs, you'll see some favorite links on the left side of the dialog. Just click on your username to see the folders that I just mentioned.

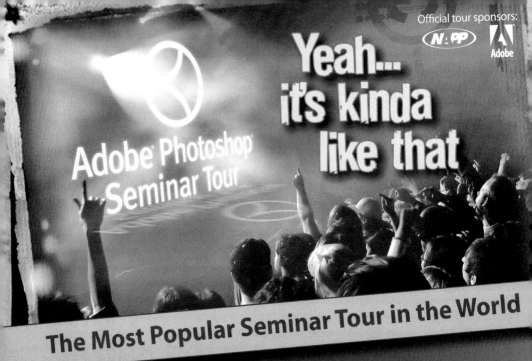